Mother Goose's
Guide to SCRAPBOOKING
Your BABY

See saw, Margery Daw, Jack shall have a new master

Jack shall have but a penny a day,

Jack shall have

Because he can't work any faster.

PLAYFUL

Aidan's playful nature manifested from the very beginning. Both adventurous and goofy, she'll always bring a smile to your face. Balboa Park. October 4, 2003.

SEE-SAW

Wendy Chang

Mother Goose's
Guide to SCRAPBOOKING
Your BABY

Creating Fabulous Projects & Pages with Classic Drawings & Cherished Rhymes

Kerry Arquette & Andrea Zocchi

cantata books   LARK BOOKS

Executive Editor
Kerry Arquette

Editor
Darlene D'Agostino

Art Director/Designer
Andrea Zocchi

Cover Design
Andrea Zocchi

Designer
Susha Roberts

Copy Editor
Dena Twinem

Created and produced
by Cantata Books Inc.

P.O. Box 740040
Arvada, CO 80006-0040

www.cantatabooks.com

Library of Congress Cataloging-in-Publication Data

Arquette, Kerry.
The mother goose guide to scrapbooking your baby / Kerry Arquette &
Andrea Zocchi.
    p. cm.
Includes bibliographical references and index.
ISBN 1-60059-004-7 (pbk.)
1. Photograph albums. 2. Nursery rhymes in art. 3. Baby books. 4.
Scrapbooks. 5. Mother Goose. I. Zocchi, Andrea. II. Title.
TR501.A775 2007
745.593--dc22

                              2006035063

10 9 8 7 6 5 4 3 2 1

First Edition

Published by Lark Books, A Division of
Sterling Publishing Co., Inc.
387 Park Avenue South, New York, N.Y. 10016

© 2007 Cantata Books Inc.

Distributed in Canada by Sterling Publishing, c/o Canadian Manda Group,
165 Dufferin Street, Toronto, Ontario, Canada M6K 3H6

Distributed in the United Kingdom by GMC Distribution Services,
Castle Place, 166 High Street, Lewes, East Sussex, England BN7 1XU

Distributed in Australia by Capricorn Link (Australia) Pty Ltd.,
P.O. Box 704, Windsor, NSW 2756 Australia

If you have questions or comments about this book,
please contact: Lark Books, 67 Broadway, Asheville, NC 28801.
Tel: (828) 253-0467

Manufactured in China

ISBN 13: 978-1-60059-004-7
ISBN 10: 1-60059-004-7

For information about custom editions, special sales, premium and
corporate purchases, please contact Sterling Special Sales Department
at 800-805-5489 or specialsales@sterlingpub.com.

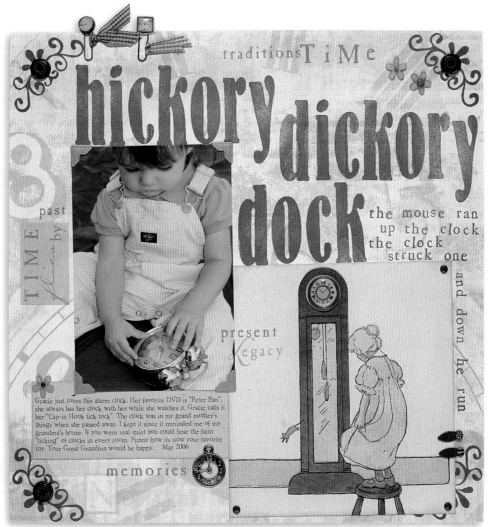

Johanna Peterson

e dedicate this book to you and to all the mothers and fathers who have delighted their children with the words, rhythm and images of these classic rhymes over the last century. And we dedicate it to their children who read the poems to their own babies. And to those babies who grew to read the Mother Goose verses to the next generation. And so it goes…

Kerry & Andrea

Table of Contents

Introduction

other Goose rhymes have been illustrated by many talented artists throughout the decades. One of the most popular artists is Blanche Fisher Wright, whose stunning drawings are now in the public domain. Wright's illustrations appear throughout this book in a variety of ways. Artists from around the country have scanned the illustrations and turned them into stunning scrapbook papers, tags, illustrations and other elements. They have then used them, along with the corresponding rhymes, on featured scrapbook pages. Other illustrations appear on book pages where they are paired with scrapbook layouts that share similar themes. Beloved Mother Goose rhymes appear throughout the book, making it a fun read for both scrapbooking parents and their children.

In addition to stunning scrapbook pages, *Mother Goose's Guide to Scrapbooking Your Baby* includes unique projects that take scrapbooking off of the page while utilizing some of Wright's most popular images. You'll find how-to directions and illustrations for creating hankies, clocks, keepsake boxes, coat pegs, baby announcements, door knob hangers, ABC baby bookends, altered flowerpots and much, much more. Make these projects for you and your little one to enjoy, or give them as one-of-a-kind baby gifts to friends and family.

Mother Goose's Guide to Scrapbooking Your Baby is filled with scrapbooking information about everything from layout and design to stamping and creating your own embellishments. Fascinating sidebars offer insights into the origins and history of Mother Goose rhymes.

Turn to the back of the book and you'll find six pages of Wright's Mother Goose illustrations. Cut them out and use them on your own scrapbook layouts. Or scan and print them so you can use them again and again. Let your creativity run wild as you explore unique ways to incorporate these delightful illustrations into your artwork. Enjoy!

Becky Teichmiller

Old Mother Goose

Old Mother Goose, when
*   She wanted to wander,*
Would ride through the air
*   On a very fine gander.*

Who Was Mother Goose?

ay the words "Mother Goose," and an image jumps into your head of a gray-haired old woman rocking gently in her chair. Around her feet, young children sit, earnestly waiting to hear another wonderful verse. Or perhaps you picture an actual goose with a beak stretched into a smile, happily quacking out stories to her brood of goslings. But who was the real Mother Goose and what inspired her to write so many memorable poems?

Some believe that Mother Goose was actually the Queen of Sheba or Queen Bertha who lived in 783 AD and was said to have had an odd, webbed foot, earning her the nickname "Queen Goose-foot." Queen Bertha is said to have loved children. She spun and sewed while telling them tales.

American historians say that Mother Goose was probably an American named Elizabeth Foster who lived more than 300 years ago. Elizabeth married Isaac Goose, and they had 16 children. One of those children was a girl named Elizabeth, after her mother. Young Elizabeth married a printer named Thomas who published a book of nursery stories called *Songs for the Nursery, or Mother Goose's Melodies*. These stories are,

we are told, the same ones that Mother Elizabeth Goose had told her children as they were growing up. A copy of Thomas' book does not exist today; however, a copy of another book, *Tales of My Mother Goose*, written by a Frenchman in the late 1600s, does exist. That book contains popular fairy tales such as Red Riding Hood, Sleeping Beauty and Tom Thumb.

While we may never know who the real Mother Goose was, we do know that the rhymes that appear in Mother Goose books were created by a number of people. Scholars argue over the identities of the authors and the true meaning of the rhymes. Both are difficult to prove because the poems were written so many years ago, but historians can make strong guesses based on their research.

Mother Goose rhymes were written for a variety of reasons. Some were riddles, some teaching tools, others were created strictly to entertain. And many were statements on politics and tales of historical events.

No matter what their origin, children and parents alike love Mother Goose rhymes. The silly words and catchy rhythms make them fun to chant. So, gather close and allow us to share some of our favorites...

Scrapbooking Supplies

Building a scrapbook page begins with the desire and the creative concept. But without the supplies, there can be nothing to admire. When you are first filling the shelves and bins in your crop room, be sure to purchase enough of the following products.

Albums

Albums protect and organize your scrapbook pages. There are all types of styles and sizes of albums, not to mention binding mechanisms, and there are pros and cons associated with each. No matter what album you choose, be sure it is of archival quality (acid-, lignin- and PVC-free).

Paper

There is a dizzying selection of papers available. Stock up on colored card-stocks that you can use to form page backgrounds, mats and journaling blocks. Patterned papers are often best to purchase by the sheet once you've decided on a page theme and palette.

Embellishments

Embroidery thread, beads, charms, die cuts, stickers, brads, eyelets, frames and other decorative elements add dimension, shine and visual interest to scrapbook pages. Pick them up at your local scrapbooking or hobby store, or raid your jewelry box, browse thrift stores and fabric stores for cool additions to your artwork.

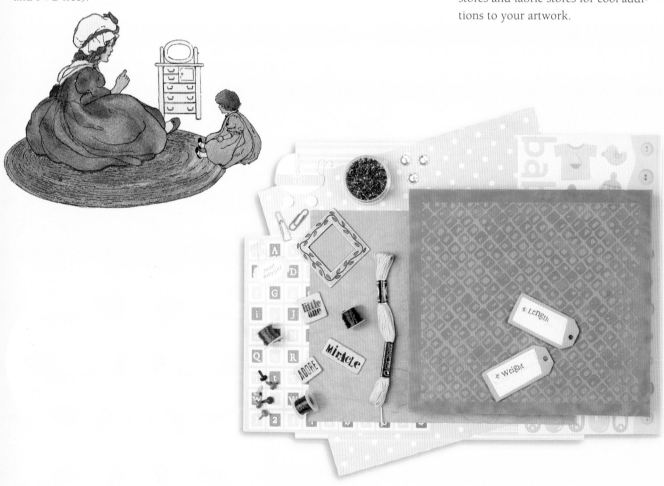

Colorants

Scrapbookers have been known to employ acrylic paint, inks, colored pencils, chalks, pens, stains and more to bring pages to life with color. Use colorants to highlight journaling, create penwork, add shading to art and emphasis to page elements.

Cutting tools

The most basic cutting tools for scrapbookers are scissors and the craft knife. Paper trimmers are excellent additions to your tool collection and can't be beat when you need to make long, clean cuts. Decorative-edged scissors, punches, nested cutting templates and a circle cutter are perks to add as you go along.

Adhesive

Choosing the correct adhesive for your scrapbook often boils down to preference. Both wet and dry adhesives are available. Glue pens, spray adhesive and tape runners are some of the most popular forms of adhesive, however it is necessary to take into consideration the size and weight of your elements before determining the best way to mount them in your album.

Miranda Ferski

Pussy-Cat and the Queen

"Pussy-cat, pussy-cat,
Where have you been?"
"I've been to London
To look at the Queen."
"Pussy-cat, pussy-cat,
What did you there?"
"I frightened a little mouse
Under the chair."

It is awful enough to find a mouse skittering across your kitchen floor or hiding in the corner of your sink cabinet, but can you imagine how upsetting it would be to find a mouse happily tucked away in the fabric of your skirt?! Well, when Queen Elizabeth I of England (1533-1603) reigned, the fashion for women was to wear dresses with enormous skirts reaching to the floor. It is said that this rhyme tells the story of the day the queen discovered a mouse lurking in the folds of her gown. The cat had his work cut out after that, keeping a keen eye on all mousy activities so the ruler wouldn't suffer further shock.

Decorative Coat Rack

Baby needs her coat for those occasions when she visits the queen or playmates at the park. Keep her jacket ready by displaying it on this wonderfully decorated rack.

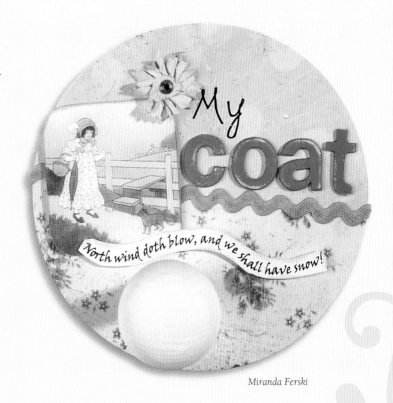

Miranda Ferski

Fancy Coat Rack

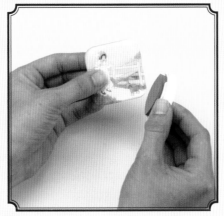

1. Cover the plaque with a base coat of paint. Once dry, lay the plaque facedown on top of patterned paper. Trace and cut it out. Adhere the paper to the plaque with decoupage medium.

2. Print artwork and journaling to size and print. Cut out both and ink the edges.

3. Paint chipboard letters green. Once dry, add them to the plaque and finish embellishing with rub-ons, flowers and rhinestones.

imes could be hard in England long ago. When crops failed, farmers were forced to turn to begging. Thousands of these desperate, rag-covered people wandered from town to town, sleeping in alleyways and on doorsteps. When the townsfolk were less than charitable, the beggars would steal what they needed, so townsfolk grew frightened. When the cry went out that "the beggars are coming to town!" children were hurried inside and weapons prepared. But who was the beggar in the velvet gown? Some say that this line criticizes the church's abbots and priors. Sworn to live simple, humble lives, many had instead grown powerful and wealthy, making the lives of the poor townsfolk even more miserable. So, while the villagers may have been frightened of the ragged beggars, they were more frightened of the rich churchmen.

Patti Hozack

Hark! Hark!

Hark, hark! the dogs do bark! Beggars are coming to town:
Some in jags, and some in rags, And some in velvet gown.

Pretty Patterned Paper Mixing

Mixing pattern paper can result in truly spectacular layouts, or layouts that seem utterly chaotic and disjointed.

Investment Theme papers, script papers, patterned papers, presorted paper packages

Pointers Select one paper with a larger print pattern. Buy five or six additional papers with smaller prints. Papers should share a common palette.

Get Fancy Rip papers or cut them into blocks, layer to create a background, use one of the papers to mat photos and another to mat a title or journaling block.

Extra, Extra Chalk torn patterned paper edges with hot shades to add energy, run patterns vertically as well as horizontally, tilt patterns for interest.

Come Out to Play

Girls and boys, come out to play,
The moon doth shine as bright as day;
Leave your supper, and leave your sleep,
And come with your play fellows into the street.
Come with a whoop, come with a call,
Come with a good will or not at all.
Up the ladder and down the wall,
A half-penny roll will serve us all.
You find milk, and I'll find flour,
And we'll have a pudding in half an hour.

Wendy Chang

Banbury Cross

Ride a cock-horse to Banbury Cross, To see an old lady upon a white horse.
Rings on her fingers, and bells on her toes, She shall have music wherever she goes.

Wendy Chang, Photo: Michelle Lewis

he mysterious horsewoman of this poem is said by some to have been Lady Godiva (1040-1080), a noblewoman who rode naked through the streets of Coventry, a town in central England, in an effort to shame her husband into lowering the taxes he imposed on the townsfolk. Others say the horsewoman was Queen Elizabeth I (1533-1603). Either woman would have owned rings to spare, and bells on the toes were, at certain times in history, a popular shoe decoration. The term "cock-horse" can either refer to an especially fine animal or the spare horse that may be attached to the front of a team in order to help pull a carriage up a steep hill. Banbury, England, once boasted a large cross in the middle of town. However, late in the 15th or early in the 16th century, Banbury's Protestant residents tore down the cross to protest the then-unpopular Catholic religion.

Baby Stationery Cards

What a lovely baby gift! Select your favorite Mother Goose illustration to include on your project. Add the rhyme or personalize the stationery with the baby's name or a catchy phrase.

Wendy Chang

Birth Announcement Variation

There are many ways to utilize Mother Goose illustrations on birth announcements. This lovely card was created by scanning the image and adjusting the transparency to 25 percent before printing on a card. The text is printed on vellum and overlaid on the illustration.

Customized Baby Cards

1. Scan and size the Mother Goose image to the desired size (ours is approximately 1.25x 1.75˝). Create multiple copies of the image using your computer software program. Print the multiple copies of images.

2. Cut out the images, and mat each on white card-stock.

3. Mount the images on homemade or store-bought card backing. Stamp the gold monogram on the lower portion of each piece of stationery.

4. Fold a strip of scrap paper all the way around the edges of the card and secure it on the back.

Clap Handies

Clap, clap handies, Mammie's wee, wee ain:
Clap, clap handies, Daddie's comin' hame,

Hame till his bonny wee bit laddie;
Clap, clap handies, My wee, wee ain.

remember this

August 6, 2001

I Love You

h a l l i e

This is the moment Hallie discovered her hands. She was sitting in the grass petting the cat, and she realized she was the one who could control her hands and fingers. She sat contentedly in the grass just making her fingers move and wiggle. Every once in a while she would let out a squeal of pure JOY.

Johanna Peterson

Remember This

Pretty pink paper looks gently woven, like raw silk, giving this background texture. Small and large silk flowers are decorated with tiny brads. Alphabet brads form the baby's name. Stitching, a bookplate and rub-on words complete the layout.

Amy Farnsworth

Nancy Dawson

Nancy Dawson was so fine
She wouldn't get up
    to serve the swine;
She lies in bed
    till eight or nine,
So it's Oh, poor Nancy Dawson.

And do ye ken
    Nancy Dawson, honey?
The wife who sells
    the barley, honey?
She won't get up to
    feed her swine,
And do ye ken
    Nancy Dawson, honey?

Stamping Success Every Time!

Stamps can be used to create titles, spiff up journaling, transform plain cardstock into background paper and more.

Investment Brown and black pigment ink, watermark ink, two dye inks in favorite colors, mini ABC stamp set, basic background stamp set (geometrics, textures or florals), stamp cleaner

Pointers Press your stamp firmly and evenly against your ink pad, press inked stamp firmly on your paper; do not rock your stamp (this will cause blurring).

Get Fancy Emboss stamped images to create dimension and sheen; stamp your inked image on your paper; cover wet stamped image with a thick layer of embossing powder; gently remove excess powder by shaking it onto a piece of scrap paper; hold a heat source 6″ from the embossed image; allow powder to melt and then dry.

Extra, Extra Cut around stamped images to create your own "stickers"; embellish stamped images with micro beads; stamp your image in black and white, and then color in the portions; mix stamped words with stickers and handwritten letters for creative titles.

Shelly Boyd

Made Them Cry

The bright colored cardstock, dotted patterned paper and brilliant red ribbons used on this page establish a high energy level for the layout. Rickrack forms an upper page border. But it is the row of black-and-white photos that ties the layout to the wonderful Mother Goose theme and supplies the fun that makes the artwork work.

Georgy Porgy

Georgy Porgy, pudding and pie,
Kissed the girls and made them cry.
When the boys came out to play,
Georgy Porgy ran away.

Handy Handsome Hankie

Whether it is a kiss or another emotional moment that starts your tears tumbling, you'll find this nifty hankie will dry them (and put a smile back on your face).

Shelly Boyd

Photo Transfer Handkerchief

1. Scan photos and illustration. Using an inkjet printer, print the image in reverse onto iron-on transfer sheet according to package instructions. Trim excess transfer sheet from image.

2. Apply the transfer to a plain white handkerchief.

3. Embellish with fabric paint and add lace or trim to the edges of the handkerchief.

Sleep, Baby, Sleep

Sleep, baby, sleep,
Our cottage vale is deep:
The little lamb in on the green,
With woolly fleece so soft and clean—
Sleep, baby, sleep.

Sleep, baby, sleep,
Down where the woodbines creep:
Be always like the lamb so mild,
A kind, and sweet, and gentle child.
Sleep, baby, sleep.

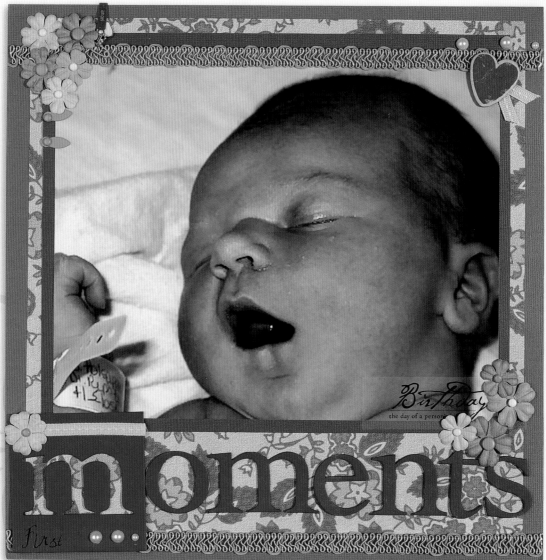

Danielle Holsapple

Moments

This stunning layout is defined by the delicate touches added by the artist. Tiny pearls, gatherings of pastel flowers, a distressed heart, pink page turns, slender fonts and ribbon seem to whisper in an understated way so as not to wake the infant.

Fears and Tears

Tommy's tears and
Mary's fears
Will make them old
before their years.

Tears can be beautiful

Tears are an expression, a way to get ones feeling out. Tears can let another know exactly what you are saying without actually saying a word. Tears can be anger, sadness, love, and truly beautiful.

Summer Ford

Emphasize Focal Photos

When you are lucky enough to have a truly spectacular photo, scrapbook it on a single-image layout and support it with page elements and embellishments. Here are some great ideas for supporting your photo.

Paper Draw the viewer's eye closer to the image by cutting curved paper shapes to overlay portions of your photo; mat the photo on clean white against a busy background; use textured paper or fabric to mat the photo and leave the edges frayed; weave a photo mat from strips of bright colored cardstock; glue a line of glitter along the edge of the photo.

Embellishments Frame the photo with ribbon; tear the photo edge and add glitter; add a teardrop jewel just inside a photo corner; use computer software to colorize strategic portions of the photo.

Amy Farnsworth

To Market

To market, to market, to buy a fat pig,
Home again, home again, jiggety jig.
To market, to market, to buy a fat hog,

Home again, home again, jiggety jog.
To market, to market, to buy a plum bun,
Home again, home again, market is done.

Sweet Craft Stick Flower Embellishments

How tasty are these delightful floral embellishments?! Simple to create, they will add whimsy and dimension to your Mother Goose scrapbook pages.

Amy Farnsworth

Craft Stick Flower Embellishments

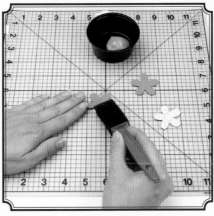

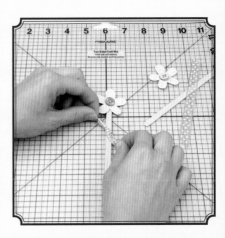

1. Cut flowers from chipboard and apply a base coat of paint.

2. Apply crackle medium according to package instructions. Apply a top coat of paint.

3. Attach the flower to a craft stick stick and embellish with buttons, ribbons, etc.

hildren who lived long ago weren't lucky enough to have the large numbers of toys that fill the shelves of today's kids. A rag doll, a hand-carved horse, a button on a string were the play things that kept many children busy. When they tired of playing with their few possessions, they made up simple games including tongue twisters like The Pumpkin-Eater. Another popular tongue twister was Peter Piper (the boy known for eating a peck of pickled peppers). Some people believe that reciting Peter Piper is a wonderful way to get rid of hiccups!

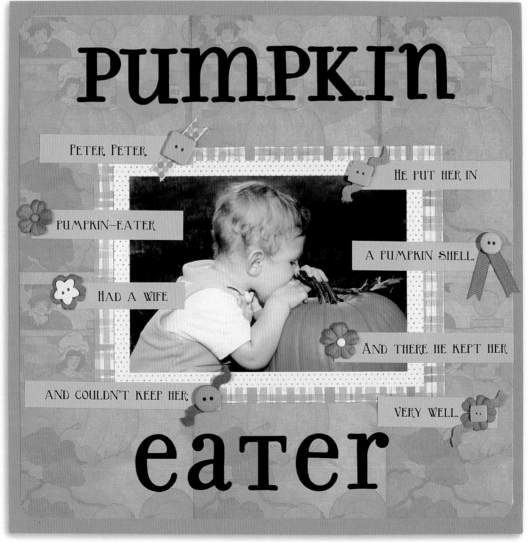

Linda Garrity

The Pumpkin-Eater
Peter, Peter, pumpkin-eater, Had a wife and couldn't keep her;
He put her in a pumpkin shell, And there he kept her very well.

Celebrate the Passage of Time

Scrapbooking is the perfect way to track and underscore changes in your child's growth and development.

Create Multiple Photo Pages Design pages that feature photos of your child taken in the same location over the course of months or years.

Create a School Portrait Album Make single-photo layouts featuring your child's yearly student portrait. Include report cards and special school memorabilia behind each individual portrait.

Journal Regularly Build pages that feature journaling. Each year ask your child a series of questions: What is your favorite color and why? What is your favorite food? Tell me about your favorite movie. What scares you? Who is your best friend? etc. Include photos of your child for visual appeal.

Embellish Decorate pages that focus on time with rulers and tape measures, clock hands and faces or calendar entries.

Amy Farnsworth

Willy Willy

Willy, Willy Wilkin
Kissed the maids a-milking, Fa, la, la!
And with his merry daffing
He set them all a-laughing, Ha, ha, ha!

Sing a Song of Sixpence

The pink background used on this yummy page looks exactly like
a tablecloth, and that works perfectly with the selected Mother Goose
rhyme. Flowers, ribbon, alphabet brads and a spiffy buckle help
balance the illustration, photo and recipe.

Johanna Peterson

Sing a Song of Sixpence

Sing a song of sixpence,
A pocket full of rye;
Four-and-twenty blackbirds
Baked in a pie!
When the pie was opened
The birds began to sing:
Was not that a dainty dish
To set before the king?

One-of-a-Kind Recipe Box

Create a unique recipe box for your favorite
culinary family secrets. Whether you are
preserving blackbird pie recipes (goodness
no!) or recipes for good ol' American apple
pies and such, you'll find yourself reaching
for this decorative box over and over again
throughout the years.

Johanna Peterson

Valerie Wehrenberg

Baby Dolly

Hush, baby, my dolly, I pray you don't cry,
And I'll give you some bread, and some milk by-and-by;
Or perhaps you like custard, or, maybe a tart,
Then to either you're welcome, with all my heart.

Ring a Ring o' Roses
Ring a ring o' roses, A pocketful of posies,
Tisha! Tisha! We all fall down.

Amy Farnsworth

his popular nursery rhyme has been in-
terpreted two ways. One dates back to the
mid-14th century when Europe was struck
by the Black Plague, which was carried by
fleas living on rats. Early symptoms of the plague included a
"rosy" red rash and blisters. Many died in such a short time
that families were unable to bury their dead, so victims were
cremated. The illness and the fires filled towns with odor

and ashes. Citizens put flowers and spices in their pockets
to sweeten the air. Before the plague was over, an estimated
one in three people had "fallen down" never to rise again.
The happier interpretation of Ring o' Roses hinges on an old
belief that when gifted children laugh, roses fall out of their
mouths. Other children dance around the gifted child, hop-
ing to make her giggle. The dancers would "fall down" in a
bow or curtsy to show their respect.

Boy and Girl

There was a little boy and a little girl
Lived in an alley;
Says the little boy to the little girl,
"Shall I, oh, shall I?"

Says the little girl to the little boy,
"What shall we do?"
Says the little boy to the little girl,
"I will kiss you."

families are

forever

This picture takes my breath away. Here you are sitting in front of the temple loving on one another. Is there anything more perfect and peaceful in this world than sweet sibling love? And the temple in the background represents everything we believe and know to be true. This picture reminds me of the day daddy and I were married 5 years ago. We innocently jumped into the real world eager to become parents. Heavenly Father blessed us with two choice spirits. We have been so blessed!

June 27, 2006

Amy Farnsworth

This Kiss

A special loving moment between young siblings is captured on this unique page. Strips of patterned papers serve double duty as a page border and title block. Elaborate bookplates frame meaningful messages. Jewels shine from the centers of rub-on flowers.

Most children have heard that there is a man in the moon and it is his face that peers down upon Earth when the moon is full. But how did that man get there? One of the stories goes like this: Once upon a time there was a man who decided to collect sticks on the Sabbath, which was forbidden in religious law. Moses caught him at his labors and punished him by banishing the man to the moon. There he lives forever. A second rhyme about the man says that one night he escaped from the moon long enough to visit Norwich, a town in eastern England. In the 11th century this town was a bustling center of commerce and a wonderful place to buy food. The man in the moon evidently purchased dinner there, but was in such a rush to get back to his moon-home that he failed to allow his supper to cool down and burned his mouth on his dessert.

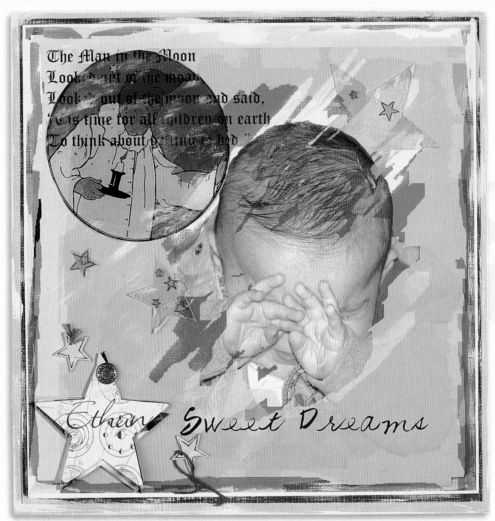

Laura McKinley

The Man in the Moon
The Man in the Moon looked out of the moon,
Looked out of the moon and said,
"Tis time for all children on the earth
To think about getting to bed."

The Man in the Moon
The Man in the Moon came tumbling down,
And asked the way to Norwich;
He went by the south, and burnt his mouth
With eating cold pease porridge.

Laura McKinley

Dreamy Switch Plate for Sweet Dreams

The Man in the Moon will usher your baby to sleep on this sweet switch plate. Let him be a part of "lights out" and "dreams on" in your good-night rituals.

Man in the Moon Switch Plate

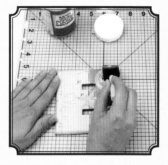
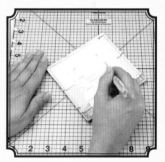

1. Lightly sand a plain switch plate.

2. Cut out a block of patterned paper a bit larger than the switch plate. Apply adhesive to the back and lay the switch plate facedown on top of the adhesive. Burnish with a bone folder to remove any air bubbles.

3. Use a craft knife to cut away the paper from the light-switch holes. Cut a small "x" in the holes, push the resulting flaps in and adhere them to the back of the plate. Use a needle to punch holes for the screws.

4. Embellish as desired with paint, rub-ons, etc. When finished, apply several coats of sealer, allowing each coat to dry between applications.

Little Miss Muffet

Little Miss Muffet Sat on a tuffet, Eating of curds and whey;
There came a big spider, And sat down beside her
And frightened Miss Muffet away.

Valerie Wehrenberg

ursery rhymes are full of "little" characters such as Little Miss Muffet, Little Bo-Peep, Little Boy Blue, Little Jack Horner, Little Polly Flinders and Little Tommy Tucker. These verses often share rhyming patterns, making it difficult for historians to determine which rhymes came first. Some say that Miss Muffet may have been Patience, the daughter of a Thomas Muffet who lived in the 1600s and was known for his study of insects and spiders.

You may not be able to find the word "tuffet" in your dictionary. The closest word you may find is "tuft" which is a bunch of material such as hair that is grouped together. Perhaps Miss Muffet is sitting on a small cushion made of hair? Some authors believe that a "tuffet" may have referred to a small stool.

Teeth and Gums

Thirty white horses
upon a red hill,
Now they tramp, now
they champ,
now they stand still.

Just Like Me

"I went up one pair of stairs."
"Just like me."
"I went up two pairs of stairs."
"Just like me."
"I went into a room."
"Just like me."
"I looked out of a window."
"Just like me."
"And there I saw a monkey."
"Just like me."

Miranda Ferski

Vicky Kelly, Photo: Valerie Garcia

Cool Borders, Corners and Mats

Borders, corners and mats add definition to scrapbook pages. They can be simple or stunningly embellished. Prepurchase them or create your own creative designs.

Borders Create unique borders by lining up and overlapping punched paper shapes or stickers; string beads and glue them into place; stamp and adhere a thick ribbon or strip of fabric to your background.

Corners Cut a triangle from cardboard or chipboard and cover it with patterned paper or fabric; cut a corner of a transparency to decorate the photo corner; decorate the corner with an oversized button, jewel, punched shape or sticker.

Mats Cut an origami snowflake; mount photos on a crocheted doily; collage a mat using torn patterned paper, coasters, napkins and postcards.

Peyton's Piggies

Peyton has discovered his feet...and

they have become one of his favorite

playthings! It just cracks me up

when I see him sucking on those

perfectly plump little piggies!

Heather Dewaelsche

Five Toes

This little pig went to market;
This little pig stayed at home;
This little pig had roast beef;
This little pig had none;
This little pig said, "Wee, wee!
I can't find my way home."

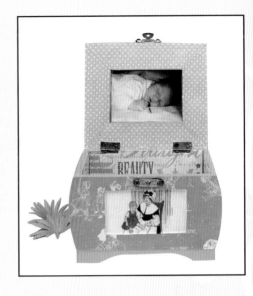

Heather Dewaelsche

Delightful Trinket Box for Treasures

This darling box is the perfect place to keep your baby's bows, pins, lullaby tapes and other important keepsakes. Select your favorite Mother Goose image and embellishments to personalize the store-bought box.

Treasured Trinket Box

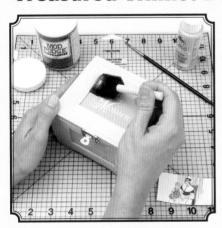

1. Paint a base coat on the "feet" and edges of an unfinished wooden trinket box. Size the illustration and text to match the box dimensions. Print and adhere the text and illustration to the box.

2. Cut pieces of patterned paper to fit the outer and inner sides of the box. Cut pieces of coordinating patterned paper to fit the frames on the outside and inside of the lid, and miter the corners. Adhere all the pieces to the box using a decoupage medium.

3. Adhere a photo to the inside of the frame on the lid or adhere another piece of coordinating patterned paper. Embellish the top of the box with paper flowers, pearls and rhinestones.

Blooming Flower Page Additions

Wedding pages, gardening pages, day-in-the-park pages and any page that calls for a colorful dimensional feminine touch benefits from a flower embellishment.

Punched Paper Flowers Punch a circular shape and an assortment of smaller circles or ovals. Adhere the smaller shapes along the outline of your circular flower center. Draw a stem and leaves. Curl the flower petals up around a small pencil to create dimension.

Flower Borders Use silk or paper flowers to create a winding floral page border, or attach small silk flowers around photo mats and journaling blocks.

Accent Flowers Small flowers mounted at the corners of photos make lovely page corners; flowers cut from floral paper can be adhered in groupings or as delicate accents to draw attention to journaling blocks; place a small flower in the hair of your photo subject; cut a large silk flower in half and adhere the straight edge to the edge of your background paper or to the edge of your photo.

Valerie Wehrenberg

Little Girl and Queen

"Little girl, little girl, where have you been?"
"Gathering flowers to give to the Queen."
"Little girl, little girl, what gave she you?"
"She gave me a diamond as big as my shoe."

ullabies come in all shapes and sizes. This is an old rhyme used by caretakers to comfort young children and assure them that Daddy has just gone on an errand and will return soon. A bunting, according to scholars, is a pudgy baby.

Bye Baby Bunting

Bye, baby bunting,
Father's gone a-hunting,
Mother's gone a-milking,
Sister's gone a-silking,
And brother's gone to buy a skin
To wrap the baby bunting in.

Amy Farnsworth

Making the Perfect Close-Up Photo

Babies define perfection, from the curve of their shell-like ears to the downy fur that covers a newborn's body. Capture the beauty of your baby in stunning close-up photos.

Photo-ops Photograph your baby's hand, the seam between leg and hip, ear and eyelashes, shoulder and neck.

How Stand back and use a telephoto lens to make your photo without disturbing your infant. Use fast film or if shooting digitally a high ISO, 400 or faster. Avoid flash as it may startle your subject. A north facing window in the early morning is an ideal light source.

When A well-rested baby is always the easiest subject. However don't forget those precious moments when Baby is asleep, in Daddy's arms, or even when a gentle tear is running down Baby's cheek.

Mother Goose's Guide to Scrapbooking Your Baby

Pat-a-Cake

Pat-a-cake, pat-a-cake, Baker's man!
So I do, master, As fast as I can.

Pat it, and prick it, And mark it with T,
Put it in the oven for Tommy and me.

Miranda Ferski

Pat-a-Cake

The delightful striped patterned paper used on this layout mimics the playpen rails behind the baby. The vertical Baby of Mine title runs up the page, further complementing the stripes. Colorful brads and the Mother Goose illustration and verse complete the layout.

Spoon Wall Hanging

1. Print and crop your child's photo to fit the curved portion of a large spoon. Apply a base coat of paint to the spoon. Allow it to dry.

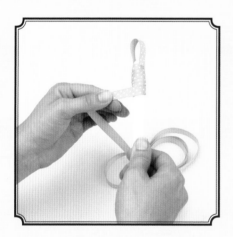

2. Adhere a short length of ribbon to the top of the spoon to create a loop. Cover the spoon handle with decoupage medium and immediately begin tightly wrapping ribbon around it.

Whip Up a
Quirky Wall Decoration

No tiny silver spoon for your little one when a large baking spoon can be turned into such a nifty wall hanging! Feature your baby's photo and a silhouette-cut pat-a-cake illustration.

3. Glue your photo to the lip of the spoon. Apply a coat of decoupage medium over the photo and ribbon. Once dry, complete by adding embellishments including the Mother Goose image.

Miranda Ferski

Little Boy Blue

Little Boy Blue come blow your horn!
The sheep's in the meadow, the cow's in the corn.

Where's the boy that looks after the sheep?
Under the haystack, fast asleep!

Amy Jandrisevits

ences weren't a part of rural scenery in previous centuries, and livestock roamed and grazed under the watchful eye of a shepherd. Some believe that Little Boy Blue is simply a gentle poem about a pastoral scene in past times. Other historians believe that Little Boy Blue was a man named Cardinal Thomas Wolsey (1475-1530). Wolsey, one of the most powerful men in England during Henry VIII's reign, was known for "blowing his own horn." He spent little time tending his religious flock, dedicating his hours instead to increasing his wealth and power. Wolsey should have paid more attention to business. When he failed to get the Pope to grant King Henry VIII's divorce from Catherine of Aragon, the king had him arrested. Wolsey died before he could answer the charges.

A Princess and Her Frog

Pages just don't get cuter than this one with its terrific photos; creative title formed with chipboard letters, rub-ons and stickers; ribbon and patterned papers. The overlapping page elements dominated by cool shades of blue and green give the page dimension without detracting from the pictures.

Amy Farnsworth

Debbie Boring, Photo: Daniel Boring

Play Days

How many days has my baby to play?
Saturday, Sunday, Monday,
Tuesday, Wednesday, Thursday, Friday,
Saturday, Sunday, Monday.

Mary, Mary, Quite Contrary

Mary, Mary, quite contrary, How does your garden grow?
Silver bells and cockle-shells, And pretty maids all of a row.

Miranda Ferski

The garden of Mary, Queen of Scot (1542-1587), is said to have been an enchanting place with tinkling bells hanging in flowering trees and a garden path lined with cockle sea-shells. Some say this poem describes this lovely retreat and that the pretty maids in a row were the queen's four ladies-in-waiting. Others believe that this rhyme tells the story of Mary (1515-1558), daughter of King Henry VIII and his first wife, Catherine of Aragon. When the king ended his marriage to Catherine, Mary and her mother were banished from the palace. To help pass the time in her new lodgings, Mary tutored the daughters ("pretty maids") of rich noblemen in ladylike ways and worked in her garden. And what about the "silver bells" and "cockle shells"? They are said to refer to the bells and shells used by Catholic clergy. Mary, a Catholic in a time when the British laws made it illegal to be so, was "quite contrary" in the eyes of her countrymen. The rhyme seems to be asking this stubborn woman how and what she is doing while in exile. (The answer is that she was biding time with the maids and her garden and her religion until she could take over the throne!)

Mary's Inside Garden Spot

Create an altered flowerpot using the Mary, Mary, Quite Contrary illustration, patterned papers, chipboard letters and fibers!

Miranda Ferski

Altered Flowerpot

1. Apply a base coat of paint to the pot and letters and allow to dry. Trim patterned papers to cover the pot. Trace letters on patterned paper and cut them out. Adhere papers to the pot and letters with a decoupage medium and apply a finishing coat. Sand the edges of the letters.

2. Adhere the letters to dowels with wood glue. Place foam in the pot and arrange the letters as desired. Fill the pot with decorative moss.

3. Resize artwork to fit the pot and print three copies. Cut out each copy and adhere it to the pot in layers with foam adhesive. Apply a finishing coat of decoupage medium and add paper ribbon.

Mother Goose's Guide to Scrapbooking Your Baby

The Little Girl With a Curl

There was a little girl who had a little curl
Right in the middle of her forehead;

When she was good, she was very, very good,
And when she was bad she was horrid.

Karen Buck

Enhance Photos Digitally

Black-and-white photos have a special appeal to many scrapbookers, and with today's computer software, it is easy to print photos in black-and-white and then add spot color for fun and impact.

What to Color Objects in your subject's hands such as flowers or toys, small elements you want the viewer to focus on, the blank canvas background behind your subject.

What to Make Black-and-White Busy backgrounds that detract from your subject, everyone but your subject in a group shot, urban backgrounds to give them a sophisticated look.

Happiness

This little guy has set his wheels spinning, and the circular shapes used in the layout design reinforce that motion. Scalloped edges are cut from white paper and then inked. Patterned paper with circle patterns forms a mat for the photo with its rounded corners. Even the journaling on this page circles the photo! It is a going-places, doing-things special layout.

Jamie Phillips

Willy Boy

"Willy boy, Willy boy, where are you going?
I will go with you, if that I may."
"I'm going to the meadow to see them a-mowing,
I'm going to help them to make the hay."

Mother Goose's Guide to Scrapbooking Your Baby

See-Saw

See-saw, Margery Daw,
Jack shall have a new master.

He shall earn but a penny a day,
Because he can't work any faster.

Wendy Chang, Photos: Araxi Dertavitian

Playful

A silhouette-cropped photo of an animated baby is mounted on one end of the see-saw in the Mother Goose illustration. The hat from the illustration is placed on the head of the photographed toddler. Patterned papers, a wonderful focal photo and flowers join a powerful title to create a layout that is almost too strong to be believed.

hile some nursery rhymes had to do with games, others had to do with work. This rhyme is believed to have been used by lumberjacks who would sing as they sawed down trees. The verse helped them keep a steady rhythm as they drew the saw back and forth. This, in turn, improved productivity.

Interactive Wall Plaque

Whether your baby is involved in play, or taking some down-time, you will want to let others know so as not to disturb. This wall or door hanger will do just that (besides which, it is just too cute for words!). Use your favorite Mother Goose illustration to customize the project to your and your baby's taste.

Wendy Chang

Interactive Wall Plaque

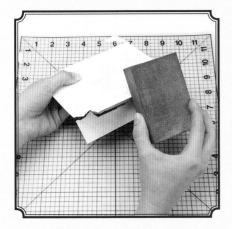

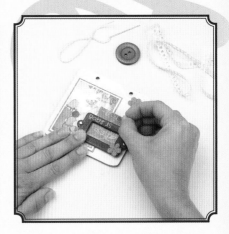

1. Adhere patterned paper to the top of a chipboard coaster and sand off the overhanging excess. Drill two holes in the top of the coaster.

2. To create the sign, measure a small block of patterned paper to fit inside the window of a bookplate, leaving enough excess on the top edge to create a pull tab. Double the length, trim and fold it in half. Apply rub-ons to both sides and paint the bookplate.

3. Print the illustration to size, mat with white cardstock and adhere it to the coaster. Adhere the book-plate, leaving the top edge free to slip in the sign. Finish with paper flowers and the button-and-trim handle.

Joan Borgelt

The House That Jack Built

This is the house
   that Jack built.
This is the malt
That lay in the house
   that Jack built.
This is the rat,
That ate the malt
That lay in the house
   that Jack built.
This is the cat
That killed the rat,
That ate the malt
That lay in the house
   that Jack built.
This is the dog,
That worried the cat,
That killed the rat,
That ate the malt
That lay in the house
   that Jack built.

Mix It Up for Eclectic Charm

"Order" is not necessarily the byword for scrapbooking. In fact, there are no "must be's" when it comes to scrapbook page design. So, if the mood hits and the style serves, why not mix it up on your page?

Lettering Create titles using a combination of printed type (mix up the fonts for fun), stickers, chipboard letters, stamped letters, die-cut and stencil letters, ticket, typewriter key and brad letters and rub-ons.

Shapes Select buckles in a variety of shapes; combine square, flower and round brads and eyelets; cut title and journaling blocks into different shapes; mount photos on multiple layers of mats of different shapes; crop photos into circles, squares, rectangles and other geometric shapes.

hy would a piper's son risk his neck by stealing an oinking pig? Historians believe that what Tom actually stole was a pastry sold in street side stands and by roving vendors 200 years ago. These pig pastries were filled with currants and sweet paste and were shaped like a pig with a curly tail.

Joshua's piggy

Sweet & Sour piggy

love

Run, run, run all day long. You love playing with your stuffed pig "Hammy", you take that little pig every where. Your second favorite thing is to run outside in the grass. You are my sweet little boy as long as I let you run outside in the grass. When I tell you to come inside for a nap or for lunch you aren't so happy. You can be quite sour when I end your fun.

hammy

Running in the grass with Hammy = Happy
Time to go inside = Not happy

Johanna Peterson

Tom, Tom, the Piper's Son
Tom, Tom, the piper's son,
Stole a pig and away he run,
The pig was eat, And Tom was beat,
And Tom ran crying, Down the street.

Sweet Slumber

A monochromatic blue background of stitched patterned papers cuddles the photo of this sleeping infant. Chipboard words are integrated within the journaling block. The frame was painted blue to match the rest of the layout. The title is created with chipboard and a hand-cut word. Ribbons and a button adorn the artwork.

dream (drĕm) *n*. 1. A series of images passing through the mind while sleeping. 2. A condition or achievement that is longed for; a fond hope. 3. One who is exceptionally gratifying or beautiful.

Lindsey has never been much of a sleeper. Ever since we brought our **bundle of joy** home from the hospital, she seemed to have trouble going to sleep. Her first four months, she would only sleep at night if I held her on my chest. During the day, the only way our **little one** would take a nap was if I was holding her or if she was in her baby swing.

One day when Lindsey was 15 months old, she'd been playing in the family room and suddenly was very quiet. When I went to check on her, I found her sound asleep on the floor in the middle of the room!

It was a **MIRACLE**!

I couldn't believe my eyes! I had to take a picture of her and record this amazing "first" on film.

I just **ADORE** watching Lindsey sleep. She looks so precious, and after all the struggles she's had, it's such a relief to see her sleeping so peacefully. Sweet dreams, baby girl!

Heather Dewaelsche

Wee Willie Winkie

Wee Willie Winkie runs through the town,
Upstairs and downstairs, in his nightgown;
Rapping at the window, crying through the lock,
"Are the children in their beds?
Now it's eight o'clock."

I'll Tell You a Story

I'll tell you a story About Jack-a-Nory:
And now my story's begun.
I'll tell you another About his brother:
And now my story is done.

Paper-Pieced Embellishments

Paper's popularity is largely due to its versatility. A sensitive hand can turn pieces of paper into delightful embellishments.

Punching Hundreds of punch designs are available, from standard geometric shapes to more complex designs. Build on a platform shape such as a circle to create flowers, animals, landscape scenes and much more.

Paper Tearing Tear shapes and piece them together; roll paper edges or pop up portions of your work with foam spacers.

Embellishing Colorize portions of your paper-pieced artwork; add tiny jewels (for eyes or a splendid collar); add glitter for sheen or penwork such as tiny faux stitch lines for visual interest.

Carolyn Cleveland, Photo: Melissa Tatarski

Mother Goose's Guide to Scrapbooking Your Baby

Little Nanny Etticoat in a white petticoat, and a red nose; The longer she stands, the shorter she grows.

Lindsey was captivated by the candle on her first birthday cake. She was completely mesmerized as she watched the glowing flame. I was afraid that she might try to reach out and touch it, so I kept my hand on her arm while we sang "Happy Birthday"!

Heather Dewaelsche

A Candle
*Little Nanny Etticoat
In a white petticoat,
And a red nose;
The longer she stands
The shorter she grows.*

Riddles have long been a form of entertainment for children, and Mother Goose was a master of this art. Some of the most clever Mother Goose riddles include these!

1. Read my riddle, I pray. What God never sees, What the king seldom sees, What we see every day.

2. As round as an apple, As deep as a cup, And all the king's horses can't fill it up.

3. Lives in winter, Dies in summer, And grows with its roots upward!

4. I went to the wood and got it, I sat me down to look for it, And brought it home because I couldn't find it.

5. Over the water, And under the water, And always with its head down.

1. An Equal, 2. A Well, 3. An Icicle, 4. A Thorn, 5. A Ship's Nail

Darling Designer Lampshade

1. Disassemble the mini lampshade. Trace the lampshade liner on the backside of patterned paper and cut it out. Adhere the paper to the lampshade liner with spray adhesive.

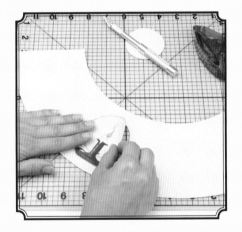

2. Size the illustration to match the lamp dimensions and cut it out. Measure the yellow "glow circle" on the illustration and use the measurements to cut a circle slightly smaller in the shade. Line up the illustration so the "glow circle" covers the hole on the outside of the shade. Adhere the illustration.

A Lamp to Light Up Baby's Life

Create a stunning lamp shade using the A Candle illustration. The lamp will be second only to your little one in receiving visitors' oohs and aahs. *Note: Never allow any part of the shade to make contact with the light's bulb or electrical socket. Do not cover areas that provide the cooling circulation of air.*

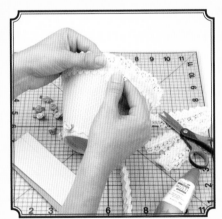

3. Reassemble the shade. Cut two lengths of ribbon slightly larger than the circumference of the top and bottom of the wire frame. Apply adhesive and fold over the wire on the appropriate end of the shade. Finish with rickrack and ribbon roses, if desired.

Heather Dewaelsche

A Pig

As I went to Bonner,
I met a pig
Without a wig,
Upon my word and honor.

Get Jazzy With Journaling

Because we are taught to read from left to right with the text flowing horizontally, it is easy too overlook the many possibilities for including journaling on your layout.

Journal Vertically Run your text up the page so that it serves as a page border, or mount vertical journaling down the center of the page to create sections.

Journal Fluidly Journal around your photo's borders, around punched shapes or die cuts. Cut your journaling into sections and mount them across your page to draw the viewer's eye.

Journal on "Stuff" Print journaling on ribbon and wrap your page in it, or on fabric for mats. Stamp journaling on acetate or glass. Journal on transparencies.

Sandra Stanton

Hush-a-Bye

Hush-a-bye baby, lie still with thy daddy,
Thy mammy has gone to the mill,

To get some meal to bake a cake,
So pray, my dear baby, lie still.

Pamela Posch

Add Dynamic Dimension

Scrapbook pages are no longer flat pieces of artwork. Today's supplies make it possible for you to create all kinds of dimension on your layouts.

Embellishments Brads, eyelets, bookplates, frames, chipboard letters, plaques, hinges, paper clips, beads and baubles all give pages a three-dimensional look and feel.

Fabric Store Finds Ribbons and fibers, from sheer satin to rustic twine lend texture and dimension to your layout; silk flowers, elastic, buttons, buckles and clasps do so as well.

Household Items Washers, nails, screws, pieces of old earrings or necklaces, barrettes, uncooked beans and peas, pods and seeds, coasters, tile chips and other "throw-aways" provide three dimensional interest.

Some say that the "crooked man" was a Scottish general named Sir Alexander Leslie and that the "crooked sixpence" represents King Charles I (1600-1649) who ruled both England and Scotland. The "crooked stile" is the jagged border between England and Scotland that separated the often-feuding countries. King Charles I and Sir Leslie finally reached a peace agreement, but like a "crooked house,"

this understanding was unsteady. When, in 1640, the Scots rebelled against the king's attempts to reform the Church of Scotland, King Charles attempted an invasion. It failed, resuming the conflict. Several years later the Scots supported the English Parliament, which was also at odds with King Charles, and eventually King Charles was tried and beheaded for treason.

Shelly Boyd

The Crooked Sixpence

There was a crooked man, and he went a crooked mile,
He found a crooked sixpence beside a crooked stile;
He bought a crooked cat, which caught a crooked mouse,
And they all lived together in a little crooked house.

Knob Hangers to Decorate Your Little Wanderer's Bedroom Door

Energetic little people need their privacy. Create a door hanger that allows them the downtime they need for rest or quiet-time play, using a Mother Goose illustration, ribbon, a photo and stickers.

Decorative Knob Hanger

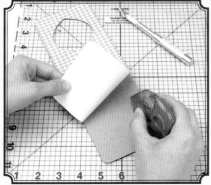

1. Cut a rectangle with rounded corners from chipboard and cover it with patterned paper.

KEEP THE DOOR CLOSED

There was a crooked man and he went a crooked mile, He found a crooked sixpence beside a crooked stile, He bought a crooked cat, which caught a crooked mouse, and they all lived together in a little crooked house.

♥ Little Wanderer

Shelly Boyd

2. Open the illustration in image-editing software and type text into a new layer. Size the illustration to fit the chipboard, print and adhere it to the chipboard.

3. Embellish the door knob hanger as desired with label, ribbon, title and silhouette-cut photo.

Unconditional LOVE

This is my favorite photo of Grandma Korf and Connor, from Christmas 2002. They always had a special fondness for each other. Even if you don't remember her, Connor, know that she loved you very much.

Nancy Korf

Forehead, Eyes, Cheeks, Nose, Mouth and Chin

Here sits the Lord Mayor,
Here sit his two men,
Here sits the cock,
Here sits the hen,
Here sit the little chickens,
Here they run in.
Chin-chopper, chin-chopper, chin-chopper chin!

Handy Pandy

Handy Pandy, Jack-a-dandy, Loves plum cake and sugar candy.
He bought some at a grocer's shop, And out he came hop, hop, hop!

Jennifer Breault

Create Movement and Excitement

A scrapbook page is more enjoyable when it is less static. Create a sense of movement for a fun and energetic layout.

Photos Capture your subject in motion (don't worry about the blur); photograph your subject from different angles or take pictures each few minutes as an event unfolds and scrapbook the multiple photos on a single scrapbook page.

Page Elements Mount elements such as stickers in circular patterns; allow portions of elements to disappear off the edge of the page; cut mats into circular shapes and use embellishments such as brads that are also round.

Mother Goose's Guide to Scrapbooking Your Baby

A Girl and Her Shoes

This little darling is developing the shoe-lovin' skills she's going to need to be a real fashion maven. The photo of the baby is matted on pale yellow cardstock and then mounted on a background of layered feminine patterned papers. The page is further adorned with delicate flowers with button centers, transparent ribbons and floral trim. Tags, a page turn and the Mother Goose illustration make the layout so special you'd walk a mile in your best heels just to admire it!

Amy Farnsworth

Cock-a-Doodle-Do!

Cock-a-doodle-do!
My dame has lost her shoe,
My master's lost his fiddle-stick
And knows not what to do.

Cock-a-doodle-do!
What is my dame to do?
Till master finds his fiddle-stick
She'll dance without her shoe.

Amy Farnsworth

Baby's Storybook About BABY!

A darling customized board book brings together your favorite Mother Goose illustration and photos of your favorite little someone. Your baby will spend hours opening, closing and admiring this sturdy little book.

Board Book for Baby

1. Use a cardboard mailing insert as the basis of your mini album or create your own. Cut a strip of cardboard to the desired size and create an accordion fold, scoring the folds with a bone folder.

2. Apply a base coat of paint to the album.

3. Adhere patterned paper to the album and use a craft knife to trim any overhanging edges.

4. Place the photos in the book and accent with embellishments.

Humpty Dumpty

Humpty Dumpty sat on a wall,
Humpty Dumpty had a great fall;
All the King's horses, and all the King's men
Cannot put Humpty Dumpty together again.

upside down

January 2006

Addie's latest new trick – seeing the world upside down . . . could it get more fun than this?

Angie Hagist

 istorians speculate that the Humpty Dumpty in this rhyme may have been King Richard III (1452-1485) of Britain, who came to power after the death of his brother, King Edward IV (1442-1483). Richard was called "The Usurper" by those who felt the crown should rightfully have gone to Edward's son. Richard's seat on the throne was as unsteady as poor Humpty's on the wall. When he fell in battle, the crown was immediately plucked up and placed on the head of Henry VII (1457-1509).

Get Flirty with Ribbon

Ribbon dresses up a scrapbook page the same way it adorns a little girl's hair. There are dozens of ways to use a stretch of ribbon on your layout.

Photo Mat Flutter Fold 2″ strips of ribbon in half and staple a collection of them so they peek out from beneath your photo mat.

Decorative Belt Thick and thin strips of ribbon look great wrapped either vertically or horizontally around a scrapbook page; slide the ribbon through a fancy belt buckle before adhering it.

Woven Background Create a one-of-a-kind page background by weaving ribbons before adhering them to a cardstock base.

Bows and Baubles Tie tiny bows to embellish the hair of photo subjects; adhere a tiny stretch of ribbon around a subject's neck or wrist and adorn it with a tiny jewel or charm.

Libby, 2yrs old

Cindy Fahrbach

One, Two, Buckle My Shoe

One, two,
    Buckle my shoe;
Three, four,
    Knock at the door;
Five, six,
    Pick up sticks;
Seven, eight,
    Lay them straight;
Nine, ten,
    A good, fat hen;
Eleven, twelve,
    Dig and delve;
Thirteen, fourteen,
    Maids a-courting;
Fifteen, sixteen,
    Maids in the kitchen;
Seventeen, eighteen,
    Maids a-waiting;
Nineteen, twenty,
    My plate's empty.

The Ten O'Clock Scholar

A diller, a dollar, a ten o'clock scholar!
What makes you come so soon?
You used to come at ten o'clock, But now you come at noon.

Heather Dewaelsche

hat silly words! Does this rhyme make any sense? A bit. In previous centuries the British word for a student who wasn't very bright was "diller." Some believe that the word "dollar" actually came from the word "dullard," which also describes a person who is not very smart. So, this "diller/dullard" it

seems isn't much of a student, and he's putting in no effort to improve his grades. He gets to school late each day, and the situation is going from bad to worse. He "used to come at 10 O'clock" but now he's arriving two hours later, getting to class just when everyone is taking a break for lunch.

Letter Perfect Bookends

Your baby is bound to accumulate a collection of favorite picture books. Keep them ready and within reach with these special bookends featuring The Ten O'Clock Scholar illustration.

Heather Dewaelsche

Altered Baby Bookends

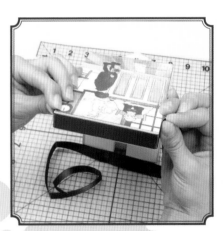

1. Paint a base coat on the inside edges of unfinished ABC bookends (available in many hobby stores) and on the wooden letters. Size the illustration to fit the inner panels of the bookends and print two copies. Measure and cut patterned paper to fit the outer panels. Adhere all paper pieces to bookends using decoupage medium.

2. Trace letters in reverse on the backside of patterned papers. Cut the letters out and adhere them to the front side of the wooden letters using decoupage medium.

3. Mount three letters onto each bookend with wood glue, placing them in a stacked configuration. Trim the edges of the bookends with ribbon, if desired.

Mother Goose's Guide to Scrapbooking Your Baby

Pease Porridge

Pease porridge hot, Pease porridge cold,
Pease porridge in the pot, Nine days old.

Some like it hot, Some like it cold,
Some like it in the pot, Nine days old.

Amy Farnsworth

Memorabilia to Scrapbook

Memorabilia keepers and pockets make it easy to include baby's keepsakes in your album. Artwork and early writings can be featured on scrapbook pages. Until you have the time to scrapbook these precious items, make sure you hold on to:

- Sonogram images
- Hospital bracelet, medical chart notes

- Birth announcements, congratulations cards, gift tags
- Baby's artwork and writing
- Baby's first spoon, fork and pacifier
- Diaper pins, hair bows and tiny necklaces
- Pieces of favorite outgrown outfits and their buttons
- Labels from favorite baby foods or clothing

Three Wise Men of Gotham

Three wise men of Gotham went to sea in a bowl;
If the bowl had been stronger
My song had been longer.

BATH TIME FUN.
INSTEAD OF JUST WASHING YOUR HAIR, I CREATED A GAME CALLED HAIR ART. WE PUT SHAMPOO IN YOUR HAIR THEN TRY TO MAKE THE FUNNIEST HAIR DESIGNS. YOU GUYS WILL DECORATE EACH OTHERS HAIR OR YOU ASK ME TO DO IT. THIS LITTLE GAME BRINGS OUT THE BEST GIGGLES IN MY BABIES!

Carrie Postma

The poor people of Gotham, England, had quite a reputation for stupidity. However, the people of Gotham say the name-calling is unfair. In fact, they maintain that they are very clever and they can prove it! Their story goes like this: Many years ago King John of Britain (1167-1216 AD) was on his way to Nottingham. Wherever the king rode, his servants and court followed, turning their path into a major highway and destroying crops. In order to try to dissuade the king from traveling through Gotham, the people of that town began to do the silliest things they could think of with the hope that the king would decide to avoid a town filled with crazy fools. They pretended to rake the moon from the sky, built roofless fences around birds and tried to drown an eel. Their efforts worked, and the king took another route. So the folks from Gotham really were quite wise after all!

Mother Goose's Guide to Scrapbooking Your Baby

hile most scholars believe that this rhyme is utter nonsense and is simply a stringing together of words to create a silly image, some believe it is intended to describe the constellations. Others offer that the verse might have been written about the goings-on of Queen Elizabeth, who was the "cat" and those who danced around her trying to meet her needs.

Maria Gallardo-Williams

The Cat and the Fiddle
Heh, diddle, diddle! The cat and the fiddle,
The cow jumped over the moon;
The little dog laughed To see such sport,
And the dish ran away with the spoon.

A Jewel of a CD Case

Baby's favorite rhymes and lullabies deserve a special resting place. Create this Cat and the Fiddle CD case to keep your favorite disc safe when not in use.

Maria Gallardo-Williams

Digital Patterned Paper

1. Scan the Mother Goose illustration and size it to approximately 2 x 2″. Create a new file using image editing software such as Adobe Photoshop or Photoshop Elements. Size the document to the exact measurements of your project.

2. Copy the illustration and paste it as a new layer onto the blank canvas. Repeat the process as many times as needed to cover the canvas. Print the design to use as patterned paper or enhance it further, if desired.

A Stitch Is Fine

Stitching on scrapbook pages helps create a warm and fuzzy down-home feeling.

Machine Stitch Stitch together blocks of background paper to create a quilted look; run zigzag seams up the edges of photo mats or borders; stitch ribbons to the page or use your machine to create decorative patterns on ribbons or paper.

Hand Stitch Use a looping stitch and heavy thread to create a blanket seam along the edges of your paper; embroider designs on paper or fabric for embellishments; embroider portions of titles; cross-stitch the corners of photos to create unique photo corners.

Digitally Stitch Import stitch patterns from digital kits for easy and perfect stitching on digital scrapbook pages.

Joni Perkins

The King of France

The King of France went
  up the hill,
With twenty thousand men;
The King of France came
  down the hill,
And ne'er went up again.

 t was rare for Europe to be in peace, and yet such a period existed in the early 1600s. King Henry IV (1589-1610) was on the French throne. For reasons unknown, he decided to wage war against England in 1610, and so gathered together an enormous army of 40,000 soldiers. Edward, of England, beat back the French king. Henry IV had no chance to stage another attack before he was assassinated.

Yvonne Hoaby

The Little Bird

Once I saw a little bird
  Come hop, hop, hop;
So I cried, "Little bird,
  Will you stop, stop, stop?"

And was going to the window
  To say, "How do you do?"
But he shook his little tail,
  And far away he flew.

Bird! Where Are You?

Just the right sticker can make a great page even better. This fun layout benefits from the whimsical birdhouse and flower stickers. A woven tag, brads and an inked title wrap up the page.

Laura McKinley

Sing

The silhouette-cropped photo of this toddler is popped up with foam spacers and mounted on a photo background before being mounted again on pale tan cardstock. The apple in the child's hand is cropped to fit within the center of a button. A chipboard letter and acrylic discs create the title. Tiny metal musical notes embellish the title while metal utensils embellish the rhyme block.

Little Tom Tucker

Little Tom Tucker
* Sings for his supper.*
What shall he eat?
* White bread and butter.*
How will he cut it
* Without e'er knife?*
How will he be married
* Without e'er a wife?*

A Charming, Dangling Ornament

It's a key chain! It's a charm! It's anything you wish it to be! This lovely piece of art will decorate your home or your wardrobe in a way that will have others asking, "Where did you get that?" The artist soldered this piece, but the steps below show an easier variation.

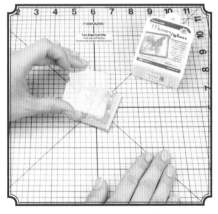

Laura McKinley

Two-Sided Dangling Charm

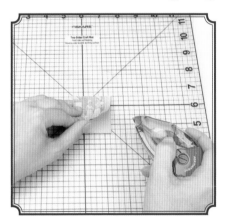

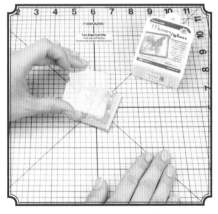

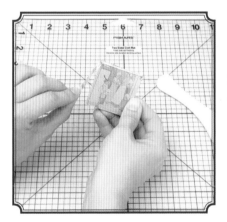

1. Create a piece of double-sided artwork using photos, a paper collage or a Mother Goose illustration.

2. Clean two identically sized pieces of cut glass. Sandwich the artwork between the two pieces of glass.

3. Cover the edges of the glass with foil tape and use a bone folder to burnish the tape to the edges.

Amy Welsh

Anne Magee

The Seasons

Spring is showery, flowery, bowery;
Summer: hoppy, croppy, poppy;
Autumn: wheezy, sneezy, freezy;
Winter: slippy, drippy, nippy.

The Year

January brings the snow,
    Makes our feet and fingers glow.

February brings the rain,
    Thaws the frozen lake again.

March brings breezes loud and shrill,
    Stirs the dancing daffodil.

April brings the primrose sweet,
    Scatters daisies at our feet.

May brings flocks of pretty lambs,
    Skipping by their fleecy dams.

June brings tulips, lilies, roses,
    Fills the children's hands with posies.

Hot July brings cooling showers,
    Apricots and gillyflowers.

August brings the sheaves of corn,
    Then the harvest home is borne.

Warm September brings the fruit,
    Sportsmen then begin to shoot.

Fresh October rings the pheasant,
    Then to gather nuts is pleasant.

Dull November brings the blast,
    Then the leaves are whirling fast.

Chill December brings the sleet,
    Blazing fire and Christmas treat.

Amy Farnsworth

Pat Taylor

Mother Goose's Guide to Scrapbooking Your Baby

Oh, dear, what could the matter be?
Oh, dear, what could the matter be?
Oh, dear, what could the matter be?
Johnny's so long at the fair.

He promised he'd buy me a bunch of blue ribbons.
He promised he'd buy me a bunch of blue ribbons.
He promised he'd buy me a bunch of blue ribbons.
To tie up my bonny brown hair.

Ava Noelle

Why are you so in [LOVE] with my ribbons?

Miranda Ferski

The Bunch of Blue Ribbons

Oh, dear, what can the matter be?
Oh, dear, what can the matter be?
Oh, dear, what can the matter be?
Johnny's so long at the fair.
He promised he'd buy me a bunch of blue ribbons,
He promised he'd buy me a bunch of blue ribbons,
He promised he'd buy me a bunch of blue ribbons,
To tie up my bonny brown hair.

A Feminine Bow Holder for Your Princess

Those baby-fine locks will look absolutely adorable tied up with delicate ribbons and bows. And when they aren't in your baby's hair, you can keep them tidy and organized on this hanging bow holder. No more knotted ribbons! No more reason for "oh dear-ing!"

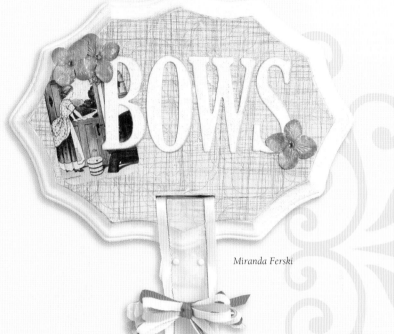

Miranda Ferski

Dainty Hair-Bow Organizer

1. Apply a base coat of paint to a precut plaque and allow it to dry. Place the plaque facedown onto the back of patterned paper. Trace around the plaque and cut out the paper.

2. Apply a base coat of glittery decoupage medium to the plaque and adhere paper. Once dry, sand and ink the edges of the plaque.

3. Resize the illustration, print and trim. Adhere letters and accents to the plaque. Apply a finishing coat of glittery decoupage medium.

4. Run ribbon through the slot at the bottom of the plaque and secure it with brads, or glue it to the backside of the plaque.

Drawing on Your Art

Pencils and pens are a staple of any scrapbooker. They are used for handwritten journaling, but can be called into service to perform other tasks as well.

Stitching Use a pen or pencil to create fine stitch marks around the edges of a page or photo mat. Create a quilted paper-pieced background and use penned stitch marks to simulate the stitches from a sewing machine.

Swirls and Doodles Go with the flow and draw squiggles and doodles on your artwork. Make checkerboard squares at the corners of photos. If you are handy, draw characters or symbols that support your theme.

Fill in the Blanks Use pen or pencil to connect page elements like a kite and its tail or a flower's head and its leaves.

Find Shade Use a pencil to lightly color portions of elements to create a sense of dimension by forming areas that appear as if they are in the shade.

Debbie Wehrenberg

Ding Dong Dell

Ding, dong, dell, Pussy's in the well!
Who put her in? Little Tommy Lin.
Who pulled her out? Little Johnny Stout.
What a naughty boy was that,

To try to drown poor pussy-cat,
Who never did him any harm,
But killed the mice in his father's barn!

Curly-Locks

Curly-locks, Curly-locks, wilt thou be mine?
Thou shalt not wash the dishes,
Nor yet feed the swine;
But sit on a cushion, and sew a fine seam,
And feed upon strawberries, sugar, and cream.

Rose Ann Prevost, Photo: Kim Kirtley

Little One

This little baby's image is framed on all sides with a variety of creative elements. Torn, inked and stitched pieces of paper, chipboard title letters, brads, tiny buttons and mini brads are sprinkled around the layout, creating balance and visual interest.

Mother Goose's Guide to Scrapbooking Your Baby

A hot cross bun is a roll into which the shape of a cross has been cut. These buns may have originated in ancient Greece and Rome where the round shape of the bread represented the sun. The cross divided the roll into four parts, one standing for each season of the year. As the tradition evolved it was said that cutting a cross shape in a bun would free evil spirits that may have been caught in the dough while the bread was kneaded. Many years later in England, bakers made hot cross buns on Good Friday. While most were eaten, some families hung the buns in their home in the belief that they would ward off evil spirits all year long.

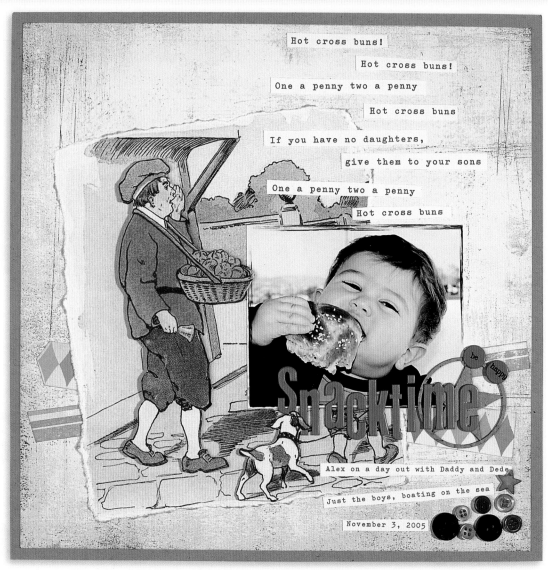

Wendy Chang

Hot-Cross Buns

Hot-cross Buns,
Hot-cross Buns,
One a penny, two a penny,
Hot-cross Buns.

Hot-cross Buns,
Hot-cross Buns,
If ye have no daughters,
Give them to your sons.

Wendy Chang

Altered Clock

Make a decorative clock for your kitchen or your baby's room by enlarging a Mother Goose image. Cut it to fit the inside dimensions of an unassembled clock. Add sticker letters and reassemble!

Hot-Cross Buns!

Hot Cross Buns to Make with Your Kids

1¼ cups milk

2 tablespoons Rapid Rise active dry yeast

3½ cups white flour

Pinch of salt

2 tablespoons sugar (white or brown)

1 teaspoon cinnamon

Pinch of nutmeg, allspice & ground cloves

2 eggs

2 tablespoons butter, softened

½ to ¾ cup currants

Combine all dry ingredients in a large bowl. Combine milk and butter in a separate container and heat until very hot to the touch. Pour hot ingredients into dry ingredients. Knead for a minute. Add the eggs. Knead until blended. Add the currents. Knead until the dough becomes elastic and a bit shiny. Set the dough aside for 10 minutes to rest. Knead one more time for about a minute. Form the dough into a loaf. Cut the loaf into 18 disc-like pieces. Lay the pieces out on a greased baking sheet. When the dough has doubled in size, cut a deep cross in the center using either clean scissors or a sharp knife (a grown-up should do this for young children). Cook the rolls in a preheated 425-degree oven until golden (approximately 10 minutes). Allow to cool and then glaze.

Glaze

½ cup confectioner's sugar and 2 teaspoons of milk. Mix until creamy. Drizzle on the cooled buns.

There Was an Old Woman

There was an old woman who lived in a shoe,
She had so many children she didn't know what to do;

She gave them some broth without any bread,
She whipped them all soundly and put them to bed.

Amy Farnsworth

In the 1500s, British Parliament, the "old woman," helped govern the British Isles, the "shoe," which included Wales, Scotland and Ireland. Like bickering, whining children, these areas were a constant headache to their rulers. They were soundly punished for their behavior by the crowning of the unpopular king, James I (1566-1625) in 1603. There was little they could do but "go to bed" and sleep on their predicament.

Glamour Girl

There is nothing overdone about this gently elegant page. Chipboard letters form the title, tiny flowers call attention to the photo mat and a frothy purple ribbon embellishes.

Linda Garrity

Saturday, Sunday

On Saturday night
Shall be all my care
To powder my locks
And curl my hair.

On Sunday morning
My love will come in,
When he will marry me
With a gold ring.

Jumping over the candlestick was part of a celebration on a holiday called St. Catherine's Day. A lit candle was placed in the middle of the floor. The belief was that if you could jump over the candle without putting out the flame, you were guaranteed a year's good luck. Some also suspect that this verse may have been a comment on King Henry VIII's reign. It is said that Jack Be Nimble was a warning to the Church leaders not to dawdle if they wished to try to prevent King Henry VIII from taking all the Catholic lands and property. They must quickly "jump" in order to get on the far side of that hot situation.

Wendy Chang, Photo: Aimee Wong

Jack

Jack be nimble,
Jack be quick,
Jack jump over the candlestick.

Baby Schedule Clipboard

1. Cut a piece of background paper slightly larger than your clipboard. Cut two smaller pieces of coordinating patterned paper.

2. Enlarge and print your Mother Goose image. Silhouette crop Jack and his candlestick from the background.

Wendy Chang

3. Adhere your background paper to the clipboard, leaving ¼" to extend beyond the edges on all sides. Adhere coordinating paper to the middle and top portions of the clipboard. Carefully cut the paper to fit around the clip at the top of the board. When dry, use sandpaper to remove excess paper from the edges of the board.

4. Adhere Jack and the candlestick images to the board with foam tape. Add the title with stickers, rub-ons, stamped or chipboard letters. Tie a fabric strip to the clip. Attach Velcro to the pen and clipboard.

Keep Baby's Schedule on a Cunning Clipboard

There are feedings and changings and playgroups and so much else to keep track of when you have a baby! Stay a hop ahead with a darling Jack Be Nimble clipboard.

Mother Goose's Guide to Scrapbooking Your Baby

Bobby Shafto, who lived in a place called Hollybrook, County Wicklow, in the 18th century, was exceptionally good-looking, and he was immortalized by the first author of this rhyme. Later, a second verse was added and that portion was written for a man also named Robert Shafto who was running for British Parliament. He used the poem as part of his political campaign in the same way businesses use slogans—to help people remember his name. Like the first Bobby Shafto, Robert was supposed to have been extremely good-looking and women allegedly died of broken hearts if their affection was not returned.

Heather Dewaelsche

Bobby Shaftoe

Bobby Shaftoe's gone to sea, With silver buckles on his knee;
He'll come back and marry me, Pretty Bobby Shaftoe!
Bobby Shaftoe's fat and fair, Combing down his yellow hair;
He's my love for evermore, Pretty Bobby Shaftoe.

Rain

Rain, rain, go away,
Come again another day;
Little Johnny wants to play.

Paula Gilarde

"Aging" With Grace

There is something beautiful about a slightly scuffed antique that has seen some life. Scrapbook pages that look "lived in" have the same kind of appeal. There are several easy ways to give your layout a distressed look.

Paper Cover your paper with a coat of paint; once dry, use a piece of sandpaper to scuff the paint; rip paper edges; stain portions of the paper with walnut ink or lightly stamp elements with brown ink; create your own "aged" paper by collaging images and text torn from old books.

Embellishments Use rustic twines for fiber accents; paint metal bookplates or plaques, allow them to dry and then sand them so portions of the original metal shows through; use pieces of vintage jewelry from flea markets and antique stores as embellishments.

Becky Teichmiller

Ladybird

Ladybird, ladybird, fly away home!
Your house is on fire, your children all gone,
All but one, and her name is Ann,
And she crept under the pudding pan.

Ladybird

A sweep of rich, red paint creates a visual
mat for the photo of this darling little bug.
Journaling flows across the painted area,
extending onto the white cardstock background. The Mother Goose illustration, a
portion of a flower, ribbon and a creative title
that wraps around one corner of the layout
complete the page.

Becky Teichmiller

Mother Goose's Guide to Scrapbooking Your Baby

Old King Cole

Old King Cole,
Was a merry old soul,
And a merry old soul was he;
He called for his pipe,
And he called for his bowl,
And he called for his fiddlers three!

And every fiddler, he had a fine fiddle,
And a very fine fiddle had he.
"Twee tweedle dee, tweedle dee," went the fiddlers.
Oh, there's none so rare
As can compare
With King Cole and his fiddlers three.

Johanna Peterson

 ome believe that King Cole ruled England in the third century. He is said to have been both jolly and brave, and his daughter was a very talented musician. Others say that the merry king in the rhyme was not a king at all, but a clothing merchant by the name of Colebrook, who lived centuries later. This merchant was so wealthy that he had 140 house servants and another 300 people who worked for him. He was honored by his neighbors with the title of King.

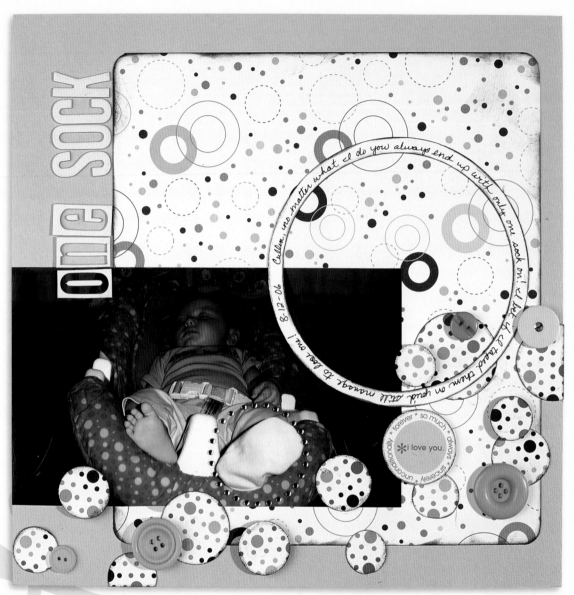

one SOCK

Becky Teichmiller

Diddle Diddle Dumpling

Diddle diddle dumpling, my son John
Went to bed with his breeches on,
One stocking off, and one stocking on;
Diddle diddle dumpling, my son John.

Punch and Judy

Punch and Judy fought
for a pie.
Punch gave Judy a blow
in the eye.
Says Punch to Judy,
"Will you have
more?"
Says Judy to Punch,
"My eye is too sore."

Amy Farnsworth

Tie Together Page Elements for Continuity

The different elements of a page must work together in order for the scrapbook layout to be successful. There are several tips to keep in mind when you are striving to achieve a cohesive page design.

Patterned Paper Elements Repeated use of the same patterned paper unites portions of the page. Punch shapes of the patterned paper to use as embellishments, use the same paper as the second layer in a double photo mat. Cut title letters from the paper or use it as a journaling block.

Title and Journaling Position your title and journaling so they physically stride over different page elements. The title, for example, may appear half on/half off a photo. The journaling may be cut into strips and mounted so it appears in different sections of the page, or you can journal in wavy lines or circles that move from element to element.

Embellishments Repeated use of the same embellishment such as frames or bookplates (try using them in an assortment of sizes) or decorative brads and buttons can create continuity in layout design.

Sherry Wright

Dance to Your Daddie

Dance to your daddie,
My bonnie laddie;
Dance to your daddie, my bonnie lamb;
You shall get a fishy,
On a little dishy;
You shall get a fishy, when the boat comes home.

Mother Goose's Guide to Scrapbooking Your Baby

Take Better Scrapbook Photos

Scrapbooking allows you to capture the big and small moments in your life and in the lives of those you love. Make the most of your photo-op moments.

Photo Angle Get down on the level of your subject or shoot from underneath. Tilt your camera to experiment with interesting angles.

Take Lots of Photos Take many more photos than you think you can possibly use. Scrapbook only the very best images.

Capture Action Use a fast shutter speed and film to capture motion. Situate yourself in a location where your subject is most likely to pass and snap the shot when she does (rather than following your subject and trying to track the motion).

Go for the Unusual Take photos from behind your subject. Use a zoom lens and take up-close pictures of your subject's hand, eye, foot or fingertip. Take your own reflection in a mirror. Ask your child to take your picture.

Sherry Wright

3-D Bootie Display Box

This wonderful three-dimensional box is the perfect way to showcase a photo of your little dancing wonder and those booties that adorned his tiny feet! Make it by decoratively painting all sides of a wooden or cardboard box. Enlarge the Mother Goose image, crop to size and adhere it to the back wall of the box. Print the rhyme and mount it along the box's upper edge. Silhouette-cut a photo of your children dancing. Fold over ¼″ along the bottom of the cropped photo and mount it with strong adhesive to the bottom of the box. Create and attach the title block. Embellish as you wish, and drape the booties over the top of the piece.

Mother Goose's Guide to Scrapbooking Your Baby

As I Was Going Along

As I was going along, along,
A-singing a comical song, song,
*   song,*
The lane that I went was so
*   long, long, long,*
And the song that I sang was so
*   long, long, long,*
And so I went singing along.

Miranda Ferski

Sulky Sue

Here's Sulky Sue,
*   What shall we do?*
Turn her face to the wall
Till she comes to.

Amy Farnsworth

Choosing Colors for Emotional Impact

Color impacts us physically and emotionally. When selecting colors for your scrapbook art, do keep the palette of your photos in mind, but also consider the energy and intention you wish to capture on your page.

Red and Pink Hot colors that increase the heart rate. They are associated with love, passion and excitement. The more saturated the shade, the more impact it has.

Yellow and Orange Colors that lift moods. They are associated with sunshine and, therefore, heat. Not as aggressive as red, yellow and orange can still be used to warm up and energize a layout.

Green A calming color, which is why many hospital emergency rooms are painted green. The color can be versatile however. A lime green is less restful than a more earthy green.

Blue Calm, cool and collected, blue is the favorite color of American men. Blue is popular on scrapbook pages because of its compatibility with most other colors, from brown to more vibrant reds.

Brown Mother Earth is settled and grounded. Brown provides a feeling of ageless beauty to scrapbook art. Warmer shades that lean toward red advance visually while those that are more gray recede.

Mother Goose's Guide to Scrapbooking Your Baby

Laura McKinley

Never Lost

The soft focus of this photo gives the layout a dreamy feeling. Layers of soft pink patterned papers add to the cloudy nature. The Mother Goose illustration is embellished with a necklace of fiber and a silvery charm. Rub-ons are used to create the title.

Lucy Locket

Lucy Locket lost her pocket,
Kitty Fisher found it;
Nothing in it, nothing in it,
But the binding round it.

An Embellished Pocket Purse

This craft project is in the bag with how-to instructions. Select your own patterned paper in a palette that matches your baby's nursery. Meaningful journaling inside, and the charming Mother Goose illustration will make this a favorite room decoration for years to come.

Laura McKinley

Polly's Pretty Pocket

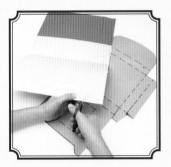

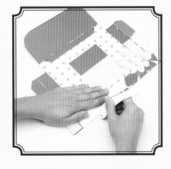

1. See page 126 for the purse pattern. Copy and enlarge the pattern to your desired size. Trace the pattern onto sturdy but pliable double-sided cardstock and cut it out.

2. Fold the cardstock according to the folds in the template. (You can trace the dotted lines visible on the pattern onto the cardstock using a stylus.) Use a bone folder to score the folds.

3. Use a stylus to trace the purse window from the pattern onto the cardstock and cut it out. Trim a printed transparency to fit inside the window and adhere it to the inside of the purse.

4. Trim all purse edges with decorative scissors. Add journaling and the scanned and printed Mother Goose image. Close with a brad.

The waxing and waning of the moon was a mystery to people who lived long ago. Nursery rhymes such as The Man in the Moon were attempts to explain the unknown. Jack and Jill reflects the Scandinavian peoples' story about Hjuki and Bil, two children who were captured by the moon while they were getting water out of a well. The moon took them with him up into the sky, and to this day you see the faces of Hjuki (Jack) and Bil (Jill) when you look up at the night sky. There they stand, on either side of the moon with a long pole and a bucket connecting them.

Wendy Chang

Jack and Jill

Jack and Jill went up the hill,
To fetch a pail of water;
Jack fell down and broke his crown,
And Jill came tumbling after.

Hill

The feeling of a fun tumble down a grassy slope is captured in the skewed mounting of the supporting images down this layout's right side. The grassy green and red printed paper is embellished with slips of journaling as well as ribbon, flowers and buttons.

What Are Little Boys Made Of?

What are little boys made of, made of?
What are little boys made of?
"Snaps and snails, and puppy-dogs' tails;
And that's what little boys are made of."

What are little girls made of, made of?
What are little girls made of?
"Sugar and spice, and all that's nice;
And that's what little girls are made of."

Diane DiTullio

Penny Arnold

Pretty Little Girl

It is hard to pull your eyes away from those of the baby in the focal image on this stunning page. But the wonder of exploring other aspects of the layout compel you to do so. Journaling blocks, a stamped title, stamped embellishments, shiny metal bows and decorative brads are layered over patterned papers. Inking creates the illusion of dimension.

Rita Shimniok

Goosey, Goosey, Gander

Goosey, goosey, gander,
   Whither dost thou wander?
Upstairs and downstairs
   And in my lady's chamber.
There I met an old man
   Who wouldn't say his prayers;
I took him by the left leg,
   And threw him down the stairs.

Goosey, Goosey Gander

When you have a truly unusual photo it simply demands to be scrapbooked. The image of this goose on the roof was the inspiration for this wonderful page. Patterned papers, ribbon, silk flowers and journaling join the Mother Goose illustration and the baby photo to balance the layout and enrich the theme.

Baby's First Building Blocks

Your little one will become familiar with his ABCs and numbers at the same time that he enjoys one of his favorite Mother Goose rhymes when playing with these delightful building blocks. Create them in the colors you and your baby like most!

Rita Shimniok

Rita Shimniok

Baby's First Blocks

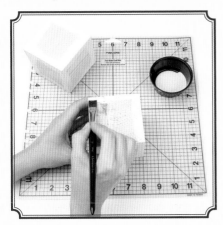

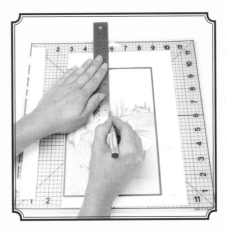

1. Apply a base coat of paint to the unfinished blocks.

2. Cut 30 squares of coordinating patterned paper to fit the blocks. Enlarge the illustration to fit the blocks and trim it into six equal squares.

3. Journal baby's basic information, such as birth date onto paper and trim into blocks. Adhere the patterned paper, journaling and illustration to the sides of the blocks.

Sandie McCarthy-Roberts

Bath Time

Three splashingly fun bath-time pages are brought together to illustrate the Rub a Dub Dub Mother Goose rhyme. The artists gravitated to watery blue palettes, but each used a very distinct and different style in scrapbooking too-cute photos of their babies during bath time.

Miranda Ferski

Claude Campeau

Rub a Dub Dub

Rub a Dub Dub
   Three men in a tub,
And who do you think they be?
   The butcher,
The baker,
   The candlestick maker,
Turn them out knaves all three!

Creative Journaling Concepts

Some scrapbook artists groan at the idea of having to journal on their layout. Find new angles that will make the job more fun.

Different Perspectives Journal from the perspective of the model in your photo, a pet or object or as though you are writing from the future or the past.

Format Use bullets, calendar or diary entries; journal in the style of a news article or comic strip; ask friends and relatives to write their thoughts and include that as journaling on your layout.

Multimedia Rip words from old books and piece them together to form sentences; journal with a combination of stickers, stamped words, rub-ons and embellishment letters.

Heather Keller

The Little Moppet

I had a little moppet, I put it in my pocket,
And fed it with corn and hay.
There came a proud beggar.
And swore he should have her,
And stole my little moppet away.

Mother Goose's Guide to Scrapbooking Your Baby

ver the years several people have claimed to be the "Mary" in this rhyme. In fact, the identity of Mary has caused quite a national controversy. We may never know who the rhyme was based upon, but we do know that the author of the verse was Sarah Josepha Hale (1788-1879), who lived in Boston, Massachusetts. She was a widow with five children and she supported them through her writings. Later in her career she became a magazine editor. The story "Mary Had A Little Lamb" was first published in 1830. Sarah claims that the verse was based on a partially true incident.

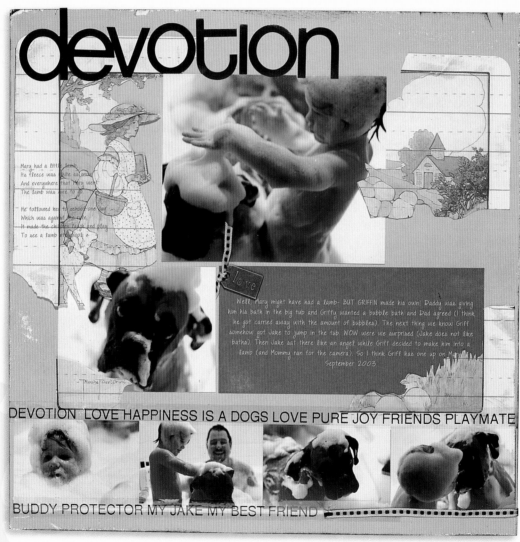

Laura McKinley

Mary's Lamb

Mary had a little lamb,
Its fleece was white as snow;
And everywhere that Mary went
The lamb was sure to go.

He followed her to school one day,
Which was against the rule;
It made the children laugh and play
To see a lamb at school.

"My First Picture Book" for Baby

Turn an old child's board book into your baby's new favorite picture book! Feature him in the story, add your favorite Mother Goose nursery rhyme and you've got an award-winning volume of fun.

Laura McKinley

Baby's Picture Book

1. Select a board book based on size and shape. Sand off the glossy coating on the cover and inside pages.

2. Determine how many pages your book will be when finished and remove any extra pages. Use a craft knife to cut out the pages as close to the spine as possible.

3. Paint the book with a base coat of paint or gesso to prevent the original artwork from bleeding through.

4. Alter each of the pages as desired. If you want a ribbon closure, sandwich the ribbon between the original book cover and the paper you used to cover it.

Amy Farnsworth

Winter

Cold and raw the north wind doth blow,
Bleak in the morning early;
All the hills are covered with snow,
And winter's now come fairly.

Big Pink Marshmallow

Glittery texture medium painted over snowflake-shaped templates can create a terrific dimensional embellishment on a snow baby page. Tiny glittery tags, a glitter-covered bookplate and cotton candy pink shiny title word add to the layout. The layout's photos make you smile as broadly as the baby in the images.

Fun With Patterned Papers

Patterned paper is, without a doubt, the most versatile scrapbooking supply. Use it for your layout's background or get creative using bits and pieces.

Cut It Slice pieces of patterned paper into strips; adhere them side by side to create platforms that break up your background; weave them to create mats; cut pieces into different shapes and sizes and lay them on top of each other.

Punch It Punch shapes from patterned paper to use as title letter blocks or embellishments; mix patterned paper patterns, shapes and sizes and then combine them for borders and photo corners.

MY **ART**
angelic

We went to the museum to see work by the Masters, but the most beautiful thing I saw while I was there was you! June 2005

PHOTOGRAPHY is my canvas and yOU my Art.

Jenny Adams Powers

Little Maid

"Little maid, pretty maid, whither goest thou?"
"Down in the forest to milk my cow."
"Shall I go with thee?" "No, not now;
When I send for thee, then come thou."

Mother Goose's Guide to Scrapbooking Your Baby

According to experts, the words "hickory" "dickory" and "dock" actually come from the words "hevera" "devera" and "dick," which is the way long-ago shepherds in Westmorland, a small county in the northwest part of England, said the numbers "eight," "nine" and "ten." Somewhere along the way, their counting method became a nursery rhyme for children who would use it to decide which child was to be first in a game such as hide-and-go-seek. The game called "one-potato" is used in a similar way today.

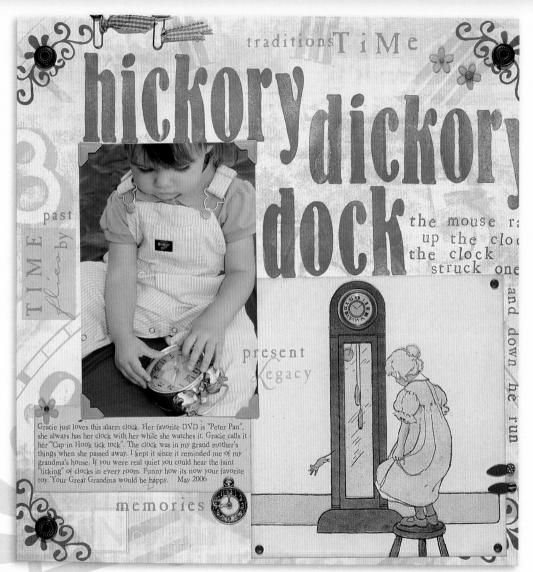

Johanna Peterson

The Mouse and the Clock
Hickory, dickory, dock!
The mouse ran up the clock;
The clock struck one, And down he run,
Hickory, dickory, dock!

the WALK

People point it out to us all the time. It's true; it's too darn cute!!! Megan's little walk is priceless. She swings her arms like she's power-walking & away she goes!

With a walk like this, she can't help but GO PLACES!!!

06/01/06
21 mths.

Angelina Schwarz

To Babylon

How many miles is it to Babylon?--
  Threescore miles and ten.
Can I get there by candle-light?--
  Yes, and back again.
If your heels are nimble and light,
  You may get there by candle-light.

A Week of Birthdays

Monday's child is fair of face,

Amy Farnsworth

Tuesday's child is full of grace,

Tonya Grieco

Wednesday's child is full of woe,

Carrie Postma

Thursday's child has far to go,

Jane Davies, Photo: Leslie Davies

Friday's child is loving and giving,

Saturday's child works hard for its living,

Becky Teichmiller

Amy Farnsworth

But the child that's born on the Sabbath day
Is bonny and blithe, and good and gay.

Amy Farnsworth

Mother Goose's Guide to Scrapbooking Your Baby

Behold a B-eautiful Wall Monogram

B is for baby, so why not B-low one up into a grand size that can bring interest to your nursery wall? Embellish it with felt buttons and a copy of the Ba Ba Black Sheep Mother Goose rhyme.

Baa, baa, black sheep
Have you any wool?
Yes, marry, have I,
Three bags full;

One for my master,
One for my dame,
But none for the little boy
Who cries in the lane.

Diana Hudson

Baa, Baa, Black Sheep

Baa, baa, black sheep,
Have you any wool?
Yes, marry, have I,
Three bags full;

One for my master,
One for my dame,
But none for the little boy
Who cries in the lane.

In 1275, Edward I of England announced that customs duties must be paid on wool and hides. Many people of the country had difficult lives, often barely scraping by. And yet, the law stated that one-third went to the Master, their king. One-third went to support their Dame, the nobility. The last third was all "the little boy who lived down the lane" was allowed to keep for himself.

Share Smith Baxter

Fingers and Toes

Every lady in this land
Has twenty nails, upon each hand
Five, and twenty on hands and feet:
All this is true, without deceit.

Rose Ann Prevost

he first London Bridge is believed to have been built over the Thames River in 43 B.C. It was wooden, and as such, was often destroyed by fire and floods. In 1176 a stone bridge was built to replace the old wooden one, but 100 years later this bridge also began to fall apart. It was rebuilt, once again, in the 19th century. Faced with a bridge that fell apart with some regularity, the people of England searched to find an answer to their problem. Would the bridge hold if it was built of different materials? Would it help to put a watchman on guard? Their concerns are reflected in the London Bridge rhyme. The more recent London Bridge was built in 1972 and stands today.

Miranda Ferski

London Bridge

London Bridge is falling down,
Falling down, falling down.
London Bridge is falling down,
My fair lady.

Build it up with wood and clay,
Wood and clay, wood and clay,
Build it up with wood and clay,
My fair lady.

Build it up with iron and steel,
Iron and steel, iron and steel,
Build it up with iron and steel,
My fair lady.

Build it up with silver and gold,
Silver and gold, silver and gold,
Build it up with silver and gold,
My fair lady.

Old Mother Hubbard

Old Mother Hubbard,
Went to the cupboard,
To fetch her poor dog a bone;
But when she came there
The cupboard was bare,
And so the poor dog had none.

She took a clean dish
To get him some tripe;
When she came back
He was smoking a pipe.

She went to the alehouse
To get him a beer;
When she came back
The dog sat in a chair.

The dame made a curtsy,
The dog made a bow;
The dame said, Your servant,"
The dog said, "Bow-wow."

Miranda Ferski

 other Hubbard was first published in 1805 as "The Comic Adventures of Old Mother Hubbard and Her Dog" by Sarah Catherine Martin (1768-1826) while she was visiting her future brother-in-law, John Pollexfen Bastard. Sarah loved to talk, and her chatter could drive a busy person to distraction. For some relief, John allegedly suggested that Sarah run along and "write one of your stupid little rhymes." That's exactly what Sarah did, and her little poem became a big success. Within a few months, more than 10,000 copies had been sold.

Mother Goose's Guide to Scrapbooking Your Baby

ind mills are used to pump water and grind grain. Wind is used to create electricity. And wind, throughout history, may have been used to rock the cradles of children. This poem is said to have been written by a young Pilgrim boy who was impressed by the way the American Indians hung their infants' cradles in the trees and allowed the wind to rock the baby while the parents worked.

Maria Gallardo-Williams

Hush-a-Bye

Hush-a-bye, baby, on the tree top!
When the wind blows the cradle will rock;
When the bough breaks the cradle will fall;
Down will come baby, bough, cradle and all.

Birth Announcements as Unique as Your Baby!

Store-bought announcements do the job—letting friends know that your little one has arrived. But personalized, hand-made announcements hail the delivery with the grace and beauty your newborn deserves.

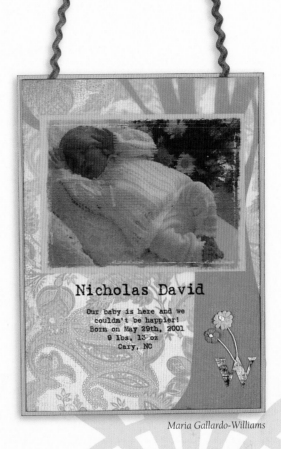

Maria Gallardo-Williams

Birth Announcements

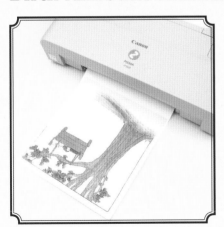

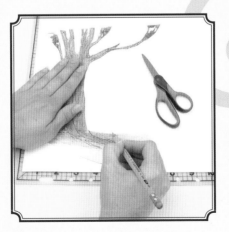

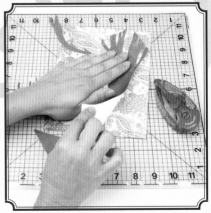

1. Using image-editing software, resize the illustration as desired and print.

2. Silhouette cut the tree from the illustration and use it as a template to trace onto the back of brown patterned paper.

3. Cut the tree from the paper, adhere it to stationery background and embellish as desired.

Mother Goose Illustrations to Scrapbook!

Blanche Fisher Wright's beautiful illustrations can be yours to use on your on scrapbook pages. Cut them out if you wish and mount them on your layouts. Or scan and print the images so you can use them again and again.

Pussy Cat and the Queen 12-13

Clap Handies 18

Hark! Hark! 14

Georgy Porgy 20-21

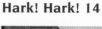

To Market 24

Boy and Girl 31

Sleep, Baby, Sleep 22

Baby Dolly 29

Man in the Moon 32-33

Sing a Song of Sixpence 28

A Pig 56

The Little Girl With a Curl 46

Five Toes 36-37

Hush-a-Bye 57

Mother Goose's Guide to Scrapbooking Your Baby

Pat-a-Cake 40-41

Humpty Dumpty 64

Forehead, Eyes... 60

Bobby Shaftoe 88

Little Maid 109

Mary, Mary, Quite Contrary 44-45

See-Saw 48-49

Sulky Sue 97

A Candle 54-55

The Crooked Sixpence 58-59

Cock-a-Doodle-Do! 62-63

The Ten O'Clock Scholar 66-67

The Cat and the Fiddle 70-71

Ladybird 90

Jack 86-87

The Little Moppet 105

The Mouse and the Clock 110

Little Tom Tucker 74-75

The Bunch of Blue Ribbons 78

Dance to Your Daddie 94-95

Mother Goose's Guide to Scrapbooking Your Baby

Baa, Baa, Black Sheep 114

Goosey, Goosey, Gander 102-103

Mary's Lamb 106-107

Lucy Locket 98-99

Banbury Cross 16-17

Hush-a-Bye 118-119

Mother Goose's Guide to Scrapbooking Your Baby

Polly Pocket Pattern

Create your own pocket just like Polly's. Begin by scanning and sizing this pattern.
See the directions on page 99 to complete the project.

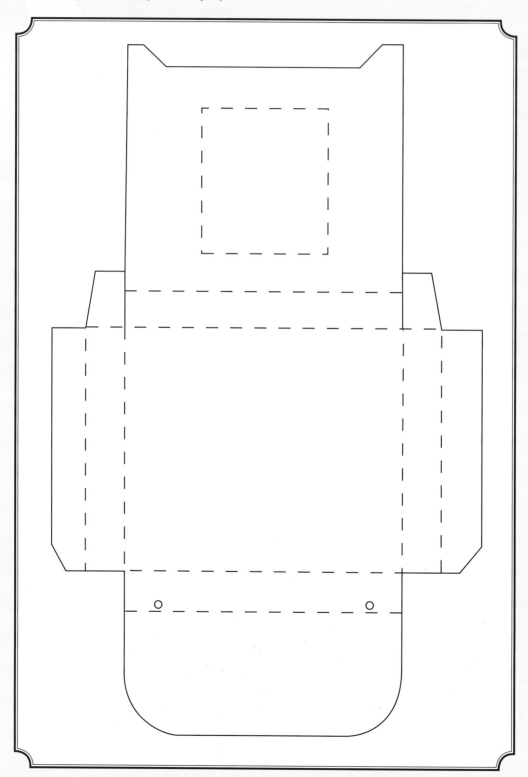

Jack Sprat

Jack Sprat
    Could eat no fat,
His wife could eat no lean;
And so
    Betwixt them both,
They licked the platter clean.

Becky Teichmiller

Bibliography

The Annotated Mother Goose by William S. Barling-Gould and Ceil Barling-Gould, Clarkson N. Potte, Inc./Publisher, 1962

Comparative Studies in Nursery Rhymes by Lina Eckenstein, Duckworth and Co, 1906

Cradle and All by Lucy Rollin, University Press of Mississippi, 1992

Engines of Instruction, Mischief, and Magic by Mary V. Jackson, University of Nebraska Press: Lincoln, 1989

The Family Book of Nursery Rhymes by Iona and Peter Opie, Oxford University Press, 1964

A History of Nursery Rhymes by Percy B. Green, Greening and Co, LTD. 1899, reissued by Singing Tree Press, 1968

Mother Goose From Nursery to Literature by Gloria T. Delamar, McFarland and Company Inc., 1987

The Nursery Rhyme by Barry Stevens, Coronado Press, 1968

Nursery Rhymes and Tales by Henry Bett, M.S., Methuen and Co, LTD, 1924, reissued by Singing Tree Press, 1968

The Oxford Book of Children's Verse by Iona and Peter Opie, Oxford University Press, 1973

The Oxford Dictionary of Nursery Rhymes edited by Iona and Peter Opie, Oxford University Press 1951, reprinted 1952, 1955, 1958, 1966, 1969, 1973, 1975, 1977

The Real Personages of Mother Goose by Katherine Elwes Thomas, Lothrop, Lee & Shepard Co., 1930

Index